# Transformative Coaching Guidebook
# for
# EFT & Energy Therapy Practitioners

# The Transformative Coaching Guidebook

## For

## EFT & Energy Therapy Practitioners

====================

*Creating a Practice Curriculum*
*to Support Your Clients to Thrive!*

## Anne I. Merkel, Ph.D., CNHP

**The Ariela Group Publications**
**- Mineral Bluff, Georgia -**

ISBN:  978-0-9961262-4-3

**Join me at these locations to learn more about my Energy Therapy Programs, Services, and Products for Individuals – and – Health & Wellness Practitioners!**

**For Individuals:**

Body–Mind- Spirit Coaching Services for Individuals:
www.ArielaGroup.com

Coaching to use N-hanced EFT & Energy Therapy:
www.MyEFTCoach.com

Energy Psychology, Naturopathy, Energy Medicine:
www.AlchemistAnne.com

Autoimmune Coaching & Energy Therapy Support FREE Series:
www.myeftcoach.com/autoimmune-coaching- support-group

Bonus EFT & Energy Therapy Tapping FREE Series:
www.arielagroup.com/blog/eft-tapping-group

**For Practitioners:**

EFT & Energy Therapy Programs & Packages for Practitioners:
www.AnneMerkel.com

EFT & Energy Therapy Mastermind for Practitioners Series:

www.annemerkel.com/practitioner-mastermind

Certified Energy Therapy Practitioner Program:
www.annemerkel.com/energy-therapy-certification

Books on Amazon by Anne Merkel for Practitioners:

http://is.gd/AnnesBooks

**Autoimmune Information:**

Programs, Interviews, Presentations, Research:
http://annemerkel.com/autoimmune-programs/

*"We Inspire Conscious Living and Guide Transformation in individuals and organizations who desire to re-access the natural state of Pure Potentiality!"*

# Preface & Acknowledgements

When I was a little girl I remember coaching a younger girl on the playground about how to feel better about losing a tooth. During school it was me that everyone turned to for advice, venting, sharing issues, and ultimately asking what I would do. I learned to ask questions, be there with compassion, motivate, create a sense of accountability, and ultimately support others to have hope and shift for the better.

Many years later I found myself being paid to do the same things in Higher Education and Corporate America. My training and experience has touched hundreds of organizations and tens of thousands of individuals world-wide.

In the 1990's I was approached by several well-known coaching institutions who asked for my assistance in writing their coach training manuals. These were published and became popular, and about this time I realized that my real "calling" was to focus on using Energy Therapy tools to clear blockages that seemed to create insurmountable obstacles, chronic emotional issues, and self-sabotage in some clients.

In my successful Energy Psychology practice I've worked with many EFT & Energy Therapy Practitioners as well as licensed Health Practitioners who did not know how to structure their practice and to support it with comfortable communication and underlying coaching principles. They have begged me over the years to write a special manual or Guidebook for them... and here it is!

I hope that this Guidebook is easy for you to use and helpful as you build and grow your successful practice while applying the wonderful energy therapy tools you already use.

I am grateful for all of my own past clients, who through the years have helped me to hone my processes so that they can be presented here in this compact Guidebook to support your success.

I salute my own past mentors, teachers, coaches and guides who have taught me so that I may share with you here.  I am grateful to you all!... and you KNOW this!

Enjoy the process!!

# Guidebook Contents

# Introduction

I welcome you to the world of Transformative Coaching. This type of coaching goes way deeper than traditional Personal Life, Success, or Business Coaching because we are injecting energy therapy into the ratio... and that changes everything!... literally!

If I call it "Transformational" we focus on the gradual changes that happen with the coaching process as it transforms the client.

In "Transformative" coaching the change comes quickly so it is more a metamorphosis or transmutation from the "old self" into a "new SELF". The difference in the ratio is the addition of energy therapy as its basis, and the change comes quickly and with subtlety, requiring the process to remain more "organic" than most traditional coaching programs.

I presume that if you have gotten this far you are a Health & Wellness Practitioner of some kind and have some level of background using energy therapy modalities in your practice with clients or patients.

Congratulations! You realize that your various modalities "take" better when all emotional and energetic blocks are cleared.  Chiropractic adjustments hold better, medications do what they are supposed to with fewer negative side effects, supplements and nutrients are better assimilated, counseling and therapy goes deeper, and coaching no longer runs into the proverbial "brick wall" with self-sabotage. Clients or patients are less stressed, more open to your interventions, and have hope that they can and will get beyond whatever is causing their dis-ease.

## Purpose

My purpose in sharing this **Coaching Guidebook** is to provide you with a coaching foundation or curriculum that you can use with clients or patients whenever you apply the energy therapy components of your practice.

You may have been trained as a massage therapist or other hands-on body worker, so talking with your clients may present some issues which you can first clear in yourself as you then apply the guidelines in your practice.
As a traditional mental health therapist you may be used to talking about the story, and with energy therapy and coaching you can move beyond this... sometimes without asking the client to tell the story at all. This is quite helpful as you move into the dark areas of PTSD and gently begin to chip away at the stuck trauma energy. It won't be long before the client is able to tell the entire story without stress or past reactions to the trauma. This protocol makes it less stressful to the therapist too.

Very skilled Health Practitioners can use this guide to provide pointers as they move into new areas not readily covered in their professional training.

EFT and Energy Therapy Practitioners who merely wish to use the tools for themselves, their family members, and friends... or those who have practices with clients, will benefit from the guidance provided here as they learn new steps that will enable them to go deeper into their own practices, using the tools within a coaching framework.

## My Credentials as Your Guide and Teacher:

With certifications as both a Personal Wellness and Business Success Coach, I have worked with corporations and individuals from over 120 countries world-wide to support clients in all aspects of business and personal health, wellness, and success. I enjoy guiding my own clients to clear all blocks to accessing a state of "Pure Potentiality" so that everything is possible to them. As a Success Coach the Conscious Transformation that I support in my clients takes them to the next level in their relationships, health, wealth, and basic joy factor. I am committed to help you support your own clients in the same way.

After years of requests, in 2012 under the umbrella of The Ariela Group of Wholistic Services I implemented the **Energy Therapy Practitioner Certification Program** for Health & Wellness practitioners of all types,[1] enabling them to incorporate various energy therapy modalities into on-going practices with patients or clients. This is becoming a popular program where each candidate works one-on-one by phone or in person with me weekly for six months in addition to participating in a twice-monthly **MasterMind** group with other practitioners.[2] The success these Certified Practitioners are having with their clients, their practices, and their own lives is phenomenal. I find that this **Coaching Guidebook** nicely supports Certified Energy Therapy Practitioner graduates to ground the new modalities within their practices.

## What This *Guidebook* Offers:

The **Coaching Guidebook** is a specialized manual that takes you by the hand and walks you through each step and aspect of the coaching process as I use it in my own seasoned practice. The steps are tested and proven effective. Each section includes:

- o The suggested chronological order of introduction of

---

[1] For more information go to: http://annemerkel.com/energy-therapy-certification
http://arielagroup.com/energy-therapy-certification
[2] For more information go to:  http://annemerkel.com/mastermind

each step,
- o Intended results for that coaching step,
- o An over-view of the coaching content to be carried out in each step using EFT and Energy Therapy,
- o Points of interest & discussion of topics,
- o Ready-to-use worksheets, diagrams, sample scripts, tools to guide you through the coaching steps and sessions with your clients,
- o Practical applications of EFT & Energy Therapy tools for you to support yourself for better application and understanding of each step of the coaching process that you are facilitating for your client,
- o References to other resources that support your EFT & Energy Therapy coaching practice.

The manual works hand-in-hand with additional tools such as audios, DVD's, live tele-classes, personal mentoring, and the detailed **Conscious Development Guidebook for EFT Tapping Practitioners**[3] that I provide via my websites, blogs, youtube, e-zine, facebook page, and individual mail-outs.

In addition to supporting you, the practitioner to offer a strong coaching framework for your energy practice, another strong intention behind this practical **Coaching Guidebook** is to support you to help your clients to learn inner coaching skills that will endure long past your relationship with them. The practical step-by-step approach helps you to activate in each client his or her own personal coaching skills. The guidance shared here not only supports your role as guide, but also supports your relationship with each client and empowers individuals to go forward using self-coaching skills to guide themselves.

---

[3] For more information go to:
http://is.gd/ConsciousDevelopmentGuide

## My Intention For You:

It is my intention that this *Guidebook* will remain just that – an easy-to-use guide to support your practice. To be the best EFT & Energy Therapy Practitioner you can be often requires that you set your logical mind aside and flow from your intuitive and creative subconscious mind. This text will get you started and soon you will follow the steps described here and place them into your own practice pattern that works for you and your clients or patients.

**I wish you the best. As you support your clients I feel that I am also supporting them through you via this training.  Enjoy the process!**

# TRACT I: Cases of Physical Trauma or Pain

This tract outlines the approaches taken by Practitioners working with clients or patients presenting with physical symptoms potentially caused by emotional or energetic blocks.

After the first several introductory sections, the coaching protocol differs from the approach used in TRACT II which addresses the structure for working with cases showing mental, psychological, emotional, and/or spiritual blocks.

The initial sections under this TRACT I can be applied to all cases,... especially those dealing with the History and First Client Session, so it is good to follow the flow and move through this section into the next.

# Client or Patient History

## Why a History?

One of the most important components of starting out "right" with a client or patient is in taking a history. Just as some teachers are notoriously bad at creating student exams, the art of history-taking is something that every Practitioner or Coach needs to understand and practice in order to get the most out of the process and make it worthwhile.

In my own practice I not only provide each new client with a detailed **Pre-Coaching Intake Form**, but I also invite them to fill in an on-line questionnaire provided by Net-Mind-Body for NET/Neuro Emotional Technique Practitioners like me. This is an extra in my practice, but need not hold you back because with a skillfully crafted **Client Pre-coaching Intake Form** you will have all that you need.[4]

The purpose of a detailed history form is two-fold:
- o   To provide you with enough data to become the detective as you identify and follow the recurring negative energy patterns back into
  - o   ancestral inheritance,
  - o   pre-natal womb experience,
  - o   birth to age 7-10 environmental programming, and
  - o   beyond.
- o   To give you cultural hints so that you will be able to speak to the client on his or her terms keeping in mind background, spiritual beliefs, past treatment experiences, and intensity of emotional resistance or physical symptoms.

---

[4] See **Appendix 1**

I highly recommend that you take the sample that I have supplied and you personalize it in your own language. Simplify and tailor it to your specific practice and the types of cases that you handle. Allow just enough detail to clarify without making it too verbose or confusing.

If you work with body-related issues and are a Health Practitioner you may wish to add more specific health-related questions. If you come from strictly a mental/ emotional/ spiritual practice base, then you may wish to remove the body diagrams and questions about diet and supplements/ medications. Your practice is specific and relates to your specific client or patient, so you know best which questions will help you to be the best Energy Therapy Coach Detective!

And, the importance of this is that I find that using a good and familiar (to me) Intake Form saves lots of time in a first session and allows me to do some work before I even meet with the client. And, in answering my questions the new client is better able to focus on possible causes, consistency and characteristics of recurring symptoms in their lives, and it reinforces that you are truly interested in knowing about them in order to better help them feel better.

## Practitioner – Client Agreement

And, as you are just getting started, you may wish to create and use a Contract or Agreement form with your clients. You can see the sample that I use.[5]

---

[5] See **Appendix 2**

# First Client Session

## What is the Session Priority?

We all realize by now (hopefully) that the body's priority comes first when you are using Energy Therapy tools. What the client wants to accomplish in a session may not be the highest priority or the next "layer to be peeled off" according to the body, subconscious, or energy biofield.

A skilled Practitioner will make it clear that all of the therapeutic meridian or other energy therapy work done will have some positive result – without negative side effects, however the results may not be what the client considers to be the "top priority"... and all results may be subtle and slow-coming.

Years ago when I visited an acupuncturist for physical pain the end result wasn't always pain abatement, but my sense of self-esteem changed considerably and I began to look at life different with a focus on the home life causes of the stress causing the pain.

If your client seems impatient or confused with your explanations, then have him or her tap on the EFT Eyebrow points to dissolve the emotional resistance before you begin. This will greatly help to clear these particular emotions.[6]


## Discussing the History Intake Forms:

After your client has filled in the initial Pre-coaching Intake Forms you have some valuable tools with much information... so during this first session you can clarify by asking for more information, details, dates, ages, who was involved, etc. Keep

---

[6] See **Appendix 3**

in mind the following as you do this, however:

It is not your job as a coach or Energy Therapy Practitioner to listen to the client give his or her entire life history... or even the "gory" details around a traumatic event. You must protect both yourself and your client from the energy involved in deeply emotional memories... and the details are usually not necessary.

It is your job to stay in the present and guide your client forward into the future... not dwell on the past or unearth more via your questioning when the subconscious may not yet be ready.

I always urge my clients to tap on the "heart center" or EFT Karate Chop Point as we talk about the history. This engages the subconscious and biofield along with the logical mind, and it begins the energetic clearing process while you are casually talking and getting to know each other better.

In order to protect yourself from the energy of your client, I advise that you tap along with your client – whether you are working in person or by phone. This keeps your energy field clean and protects your own health and well-being.

## Focus on the Issue or Pain:

It is best in a first session to share information, get to know the client, and start to clear their barriers to health and wellbeing... all in your limited session time.

Because I ask my clients to start tapping while we're still talking about the history, I know they are starting to get benefits and that their subconscious mind will start sharing more information about blocks. I also make it clear to the client that this is going on so that they feel like something is happening while we are talking.

If a client is suffering from acute anxiety, physical or emotional pain, or other strong symptoms, I feel strongly that it is important to start the process of clearing. And, the first step in this is to identify what the client feels is their chief complaint.

You may have this in the client history, but it is good to ask again in the session. From this you will learn the up-to-date issues that you can start to work with in the moment. And, as the energy continues to shift after a session, a new breakthrough or trigger might show up just before the next session, so it is good to keep your finger on the client's emotional pulse.


## Gauging the Charge:

Next, ask them to gauge the charge on that issue on a scale of 0 to 10..

0= No Charge/ Neutral...   5=Medium Charge...   10=Extreme High Charge!

Often a client or patient cannot really decide on a specific emotion that they are feeling related to an issue or physical pain, but they feel a sense of agitation, stuckness, blocked energy flow, or a physical sensation such as dull pain, tingling, etc. Their charge need not be labeled with an emotion... just go after the basic level of charge. Go with the client's first reaction – don't let them logically try to "figure it out" or you'll never get a gauge from which to start your session.

As you recognize the issue and its intensity, you may begin to de-charge the initial resistance now and then go deeper later (in a longer session) or in the next session.

## What Tools Should I Use?

You utilize specific tools in your practice, so you will know what you feel is best in each case. For more understanding of how to apply a basic "Coaching" foundation to your work with your client you will find all you need to know in the **TRACT II** section of this book.

# Meridian Tapping

## Meridian Tapping Techniques De-bunked:  A History

Over twenty years ago *Gary Craig*,[7] and *Dr. Scott Walker*,[8] originators of the **EFT** and **NET** techniques respectively, decided that both physical problems and psychological / behavioral issues could be cleared using tools that neutralize the emotional factors that can cause:
- o physical, emotional, psychological pain,
- o immune weakness and debilitating stress and dis-ease,
- o energetic blockages to wellness, success, happiness,
- o disruptive behavioral patterns, addictions, depression,
- o post traumatic stress syndrome,
- o among other blocks to optimum performance and peak health.

**Emotional Freedom Technique** is a form of psychological acupressure that uses a gentle tapping technique instead of needles to stimulate traditional acupuncture points. The **EFT** protocol *balances the energy system* and appears to aid psychological stress and physical pain relief. Restoring the balance of the energy system allows the body and mind to resume their natural healing abilities. **EFT** is non-invasive and is easy to learn and apply for yourself.

**EFT** was developed in the early 1980's by Gary Craig, based on the discoveries of Dr. John Diamond - a medical doctor and energy researcher; Dr. George Goodheart - a chiropractor and father of the field of Kinesiology; and Dr. Roger Callahan - a clinical psychologist. The work of these men revealed that emotional charge is stored in the body's energy system. When the energy system is cleared or balanced, the symptoms of

---

[7] For more information go to:  http://emofree.com
[8] For more information go to:  http://netmindbody.com

this emotional charge disappears - usually permanently!

**Neuro Emotional Technique** is a ***mind-body stress reduction intervention*** aimed at improving behavioral and physical problems such as chronic injuries, pain, worry, anxiety, depression, addictions, etc. This technique has diagnostic aspects and requires a trained practitioner to facilitate. The **NET** client receives a complete wholistic analysis of what issue is causing pain, where it has been stored, and what other issues might be involved. Major life changes can occur in just one session without reliving the pain of emotional events.

**NET** is a more sophisticated diagnostic and energy treatment tool than EFT and is used by licensed health facilitators world-wide to first identify whether an issue is based on:

- o   emotions,
- o   toxins/ pollutants,
- o   biochemistry/ nutrition, or
- o   physical structure.

When this is identified, the NET protocol then addresses and is used to clear the emotional causes of physical, mental, emotional pain. This tool is utilized one-on-one in person.

**N-hanced EFT** is the perfect blend, with the ease of EFT coupled with the sophistication of NET. This is what I use in my practice with clients world-wide.


## Following the Pain:

When working on a specific issue one often feels a pain or "stuck" sensation in the body. Whenever this happens it is appropriate to "follow the pain" or sensation and allow the body to clear it using a non-invasive kinesiological energy circuit that can be created by holding one hand over the location of the pain or physical sensation while placing the other hand across the forehead just above the eyebrows. When one does this the energy circuit created uses the Emotional Release neurovascular points on the forehead to neutralize the emotional issue related to the pain or body sensation. It is beneficial to breathe out the sensation.

And, if the pain or sensation happens to move from the original location to another place in the body, the hand held there must move with the sensation until it moves out of the body completely.

This is an easy-to-use process that comes from the practice of Applied Kinesiology.[9]

---

[9] Check out the **International College of Applied Kinesiology** or **Touch for Health.**

# TRACT II:
## Conscious Transformation, Business Success, and Abundance Cases

This tract outlines steps that you can take with clients or patients presenting with emotional, psychological, mental, spiritual blocks to moving forward out of "stuckness" in their lives.

The coaching protocol differs from the approach used in TRACT I which addresses specific work done by body-oriented Health Practitioners dealing with physical symptoms.

**The foundational information and initial tools and steps provided in TRACT I will help you get started in TRACT II.**

# Step 1 -Building Rapport

If you do a good job at the beginning in your first and/or second sessions the "Ice is Broken" for this and future sessions. Using your History you can ask specific questions and start the tapping away of inner blocks and resistance.

You may do some "house keeping" here where you explain the benefits to your client of filling in both **Pre-coaching** and **Post-coaching forms** for each session.[10] You can outline how you will work together and begin to get to know each other.

 In this early step of your association with your client the coach-client relationship is begun and will continue to be co-created for as long as you work together.

## Centering and Setting Session Intentions

At the beginning of most all of my client sessions I set the tone by getting centered and stating my intention to my client to "Be there with them to support their Highest intention, to meridian TAP and do energy work for their benefit, and to be the best and clearest "channel" of energy for their Highest good." I then ask them to state their own intention for the session. After that I often ask them if they would like to call in their "Healing Team", based on their own spiritual persuasion. (This may include angels, past relatives, God, Jesus, The Holy Spirit, their Highest Self, etc.)

This short and easy-to-use protocol, tailored to your own style with your own words, and using information provided if you

---

[10] See **Appendix 4**

ask in your Input form about their spiritual beliefs, is a powerful and necessary tool to use as a coach/ energy therapist.

**State below your intention of what you currently wish to accomplish in a FIRST SESSION with a client.**

Jot down the first thoughts that come to mind... only YOU will see these, and it will help you to gauge where you are NOW and where you can go from here after some instruction. Also, use this exercise as a "rehearsal" as you get ready for the first session with each new client.

*Below is a guide to remind you of the steps to center and create intentions for each first session with a client. You may want to copy this guide and place it in each new client's file just as a reminder and a "cue card" to begin the first session until you either personalize this template or no longer need to refer to it.*

## First Session Sample Script

**Greetings and Welcome to the call/session!!** (Personalize this and all of the other lines to fit your personality and that of your client. A very small amount of pleasantries may be exchanged here based on cultural norms for you and your client and the nationalities represented.)

## Let us move right into the session:
First, let us get centered.
- o Are you comfortable in a quiet area where you can best take this call?
- o Do you have plenty of water to drink during your session so you will stay hydrated?
- o Do you have paper and pen for your session notes?
- o Is the phone volume comfortable for you?

Let us breath out any frustrations or tensions that have followed us here.

Take some deep breaths and stretch your body – arms, legs, torso, twist at your waist, turn your head from side to side, make faces to energize your facial muscles, wiggle your fingers and toes.

You can close your eyes if this feels comfortable, and just feel PEACE surround you as you breathe deeply.

Think about what brought you to this coaching/ energy

therapy session. Why have you signed up for our sessions to start now?

Now we will set some specific intentions for this first session together.

I will begin the process so that you can experience what an intention sounds like.
Since this is our first session I want to first get to know you so that we can co-create a comfortable rapport of trust.

As I get to know you I want to share the process that we will follow and share some guidelines for personal organization that will help you to get the most out of this and all of the other sessions we will have together.

Now, since this session and all of our subsequent meetings are about YOU, what is YOUR intention for today's session?

[Client now states his/her intention.]

Thank you for sharing that. Now let us move forward

Thank you for providing me with information via the Pre-Coaching Intake Form that I provided to you when you signed up.

I have looked over your information and have a few questions...

After this session and all subsequent sessions I highly recommend that you fill in the Post-coaching Form for today and a Pre-coaching Form prior to each future session in order to keep me up-to-date and to clarify your intentions for future sessions. This will assist us BOTH to reap greater benefits from your coaching/ energy therapy sessions.

Please provide me with the post-coaching information 24

hours after each session and provide the pre-coaching information 24 hours before your next session. This will allow your meridians to re-calibrate over the 24 hours after our session, and will allow me enough time before your next session to study the information you provide. [**END of Script**]


*Now is your opportunity to take the above "script" and customize it for your own use in client sessions.*

## Getting Comfortable With Setting the Coaching Foundation in Your Energy Practice

When the first session with a client is scheduled you may or may not have already had a previous conversation with the person to be your client... but at the very least you have corresponded by e-mail.

It is important for you to understand coaching rather than counseling philosophy.

It is your job to set the tone and hold the space for good coaching to occur coupled with appropriate energy therapy for the client, so you must personally feel comfortable with an inner understanding of your role and how to best support your clients.

To best do this, it is important to remember the following points:

There are transformational steps to be taken on both the INNER and OUTER levels, and you will not only activate these in YOURSELF, but will guide your client to do the same. The INNER and OUTER must be in balance for the best results. **COACHING = co-creating a relationship** - where the coach is more INTEREST**ED** than INTEREST**ING** – meaning that it is never about you, but is always focused on the client in the now... moving toward the future. And, although you need certain details from the past to identify the original "root cause" of a recurring emotional block, you don't need to hear the entire story, and you must imagine the client to be living the results that he or she most desires. Always your client is allowed to be, and guided to be:  BRILLIANT!!

## The ROLE of a coach using energy therapy is to:

Be a vibrational model to "hold the energy" for your client...
without taking it on.
This means that you:
- o Need to do your own personal energy work and keep your body healthy.
- o Support energy shifts in your client as you keep your finger on the pulse so you don't over-tax him or her during a single session,
- o Guide your client to identify the baby steps to take,
- o Share processes that your client can apply personally for the rest of his or her life.

## The FIRST SESSIONS provide an opportunity to:
- o Get to know your client,
- o Create the tone,
- o Set the inner landscape,
- o Help your client to identify personal beliefs and intentions,
- o Guide your client to visualize and feel the results that they ultimately want in their life, work, relationships, focus area,
- o Identify the present "baseline" and the "gap" between where your client is now and where he/she wants to be – beginning with the END in mind,
- o Start to build a relationship – of TRUST... with you and your processes,
- o Support hope and positive anticipation in your client.

**The best GIFT of coaching** is to support and build your client's self esteem by recognizing that your client is perfect NOW – while having no judgments.

**The best GIFT of using energy therapy tools** is to help

clear charge from the past that has created an inner obstacle or inner resistance to success, health, happiness, prosperity, the good things in life!

## Practical Applications for YOU:

With the information provided through these "Practical Applications" sections you can participate more with your clients on their journey and more intimately understand the exercises you assign. Also as they share the information you can notice their self-esteem level and issues. Remember that low self-esteem comes from so many sources. Your job is just to notice – not to dwell there. Just read their feedback and listen to your client during each session.

*1- As we end this section we want you to summarize the steps you will take in your first session with your client.  You can list below all of the components you will focus on as you guide your first session.*

*2- Write your own Multi-sensory Vision for the next three, six, or twelve months. What do you intend to accomplish?*

It is helpful for you to do this exercise for yourself so that as you assign it to your client (especially those who are focusing on Conscious Transformation or Personal/ Business Success tracts) you have an intimate understanding of its value.[11]

---

[11] See **Appendix 5** for tips on helping your client to create a Multi-sensory Vision.

# Step 2 – Visioning & Identifying the Critical Gaps

After a session or two your client will start to recognize:
- The importance of understanding both the inner and outer paths to success,
- The protocol followed in working with you,
- The use of specific energy therapy tools,
- The level of support he or she can expect from you as a Guide, Coach, Energy Therapist,... and
- The critical GAPS between where they are NOW and where they intend to be as they live the results of their desires.

## Reviewing the Multi-sensory Vision Exercise

Since by now you have already performed the Visioning Exercise, now you may assign this very helpful exercise to your client... as personal (home) work.

If you feel that the client is not yet ready for this or is blocked in some way from looking ahead or imagining a better or different life for him or herself, then you have the tools to support getting beyond any barriers that might come under the categories of:
- Fear of the unknown,
- Fear of moving forward,
- Fear of leaving others behind,
- Inability to imagine anything different,
- Confusion about why or how to do this,
- Feelings of unworthiness to create or move toward a vision or improved life,
- Etc.

If you choose to put this exercise on hold until after you have cleared the inner resistance to moving forward, then a good exercise to use instead is the Personal Autobiography Exercise.[12]

## The Personal Autobiography Exercise

Yes, it may seem that there are many exercises assigned early in the coaching process, yet, unless you are working on serious emotional issues that show up each session, these exercises will provide a basis through which you can find emotional blocks to clear or simply get to know the background of the client and direction that he or she wishes to pursue with your guidance.

As mentioned on the exercise itself, this personal autobiography may mirror the personal history provided in the Pre-coaching Intake Form[13], however it can also provide some key elements that provide positive input and on which you and your client can build the vision for the future as well as goals. It can also itemize specific blocks to moving forward that may exist and need to be cleared. So, this is a valuable tool and comes highly recommended.

## Focus on the Critical Gap(s)

As you and the client discuss and focus on both the autobiography and vision you will not only get a feel for what support he or she may need from you as a coach, but also what the client needs from you as an Energy Therapist.

And, part of this examination will elicit the "Critical Gaps", or gaps between where the client is now in life, love, health, wealth, career, etc. and where he or she wishes to be in each area.

This is where you come in to assist the client in identifying his

---

[12] See **Appendix 6**
[13] See **Appendix 1**

or her strengths and weaknesses and where goals are needed as well as inner blocks cleared.

One way to assess the "Gap" between NOW = the "baseline", and the VISION is to ask the client to consider the following:
1. What is the difference between the baseline and the vision?
2. What might it take to get from here to there?
3. How long might this reasonably take to accomplish moving from the baseline to the end results of the vision?
4. And, the important energy therapy question: How will it FEEL to be living the results of your vision?

Based on the answers and conversation you have about the above with your client, you can easily create an entire series of coaching sessions that may or may not include energy therapy clearing.

# Step 3 – Setting a Vibrational Tone

It is important to set the stage for your client with these elements so that they experience a higher vibration that can set the foundation for each coaching session.

- o Learn the skill of looking for greatness and strength in others.
- o Focus on what IS WORKING and what FEELS RIGHT.
- o NOBODY can wear a judgment robe. Appreciate the gifts, talents, and uniqueness of all others without judgment.
- o Notice, appreciate, and absorb the GIFTS all around... even the things that do not seem to be "gifts" at first.
- o Hold a bigger view of life and a VISION... - YOUR VISION!

## Sample Coach Script – Intention/Content Introduction

*You may open your session as you always do, and include the following:*
- o "What is your intention for this session?
- o How do you choose to feel?
- o Do you feel blocked in any way right now? Is there any inner resistance?

*Here are my intentions and what I want to feel:*
- o One of my jobs as a coach/ energy therapist is to help you feel and grow and learn more about yourself.
- o All of us have self-defeating talk and self-doubts. Do you have any?
- o When I share with you, when I tell you what I see that is great, please hear it; breathe it in. I always come from a place of sincerity.
- o I choose to support you to grow beyond your inner resistance into that person you choose to be... living the

life of your dreams.

**In what areas do you currently see greatness around you?**

**[In which areas do you think you are not seeing all of your _own_ greatness?**
Show up, listen, tune in with your heart, soul, energy and love, and just bring that natural talent that you have into the coaching session to support your client.]

**In what areas do you see your own greatness?** (Probe for answers in a simple conversational way such as follows:)
- o In what areas do you see yourself as being great or brilliant or simply proficient?
- o In what areas are you really strong and skilled?
- o What else? Are there more? What other areas of your life, work, and family might you add where you demonstrate brilliance?
- o What have you done this week that proved your brilliance and your talents?

**I choose to help you get the results that you want.** (Now notice how we're shifting from the inner road to the outer.)
- o The reason that you hired me is that you choose to get bigger results.
- o You choose to let go of all blocks to your own brilliance.
- o You choose to do something different.
- o I am going to be with you on the journey so you will get those results.
- o And - I want you to remember that YOU do the work. Only YOU know when an inner resistance shows up. Only YOU know what you truly desire and what feels right to you.
- o We are going to get phenomenal results as long as you are willing to do the work and share your feelings.
- o You are committed to this, yes?

There are going to be times when I ask you to think differently; there will be times when I ask you to do things that might not feel comfortable.
You might say to me, 'I could never do this in my business because...,' or
'I don't feel comfortable having that conversation with my son because....

I will ask you to try it on anyway. This is because it is how we grow. You're going to find you don't have to say yes to me. I want you to get prepared to think bigger. In order to do this, many times I will guide you to look at things underneath what you want – to go to a deeper level."

***Work with the script above and make it YOURS. Let your own conversational style guide you to include the elements you wish to cover.***

## Inner and Outer Work

One of the things you need to support in your client is his or her ability to shift the pattern of their thoughts to be more intentional. If you help your clients to make changes on the inner level they will attract what they want more easily on the outer.

You need to model this for your client. Often people think they need to explain to others why they're doing a certain thing; clients sign on with you to help them accomplish their goals. You need not explain every step of the coaching journey that you are guiding; just continue to model and guide, and let them experience the rest.

Help your clients understand what they need to do in the inner process. They need to reprogram their brain and the method is easy. And, the energy therapy tools that you will teach them will help clear all inner resistance.

If you can help a client change even 10% of their thoughts from automatic to intentional, then they will shift their vibrational output in their thoughts, feelings, and overall frequency.

You can say to your clients that it is important to start changing their mind patterns, beliefs, thoughts and energy focus. Explain that their beliefs impact the results of any actions taken. This will help them reprogram their brain and start to change a tiny bit.

Here are some things that you can do with your client:

- Get your client started on daily scripting or short journaling. This is where they intentionally write out how they choose to FEEL in their day and what they choose to experience.
- First ask: "What has been bothering you?" "What has been worrying you?" "What things are not serving you?"
- Next have them look at what they choose to accomplish today: the physical task-oriented things.
- Then ask, "What do you choose to experience more of?"
- Remind your client to focus on how they choose to feel and include this in every aspect of the scripting/journaling.
- Finally have your client start looking for and recording their positive evidences as they move toward the improved life.
- They need to write down when something wonderful happens, - not just physical manifestations but also feelings. You can help your client activate more of their feelings and identify their essences.
- And, of course, throughout this process you can support your clients in their clearing of any inner resistance or emotional baggage that shows up.

## Identifying the Vibrational ESSENCE(s) of Life

Here is a short and powerful exercise to set the vibrational tone for creating a new life. You may try this along with your client. Believe me, it is potent... and it truly works!

**Step 1: Identify 3-5 feelings, characteristics, "essences" that you choose to FEEL in every aspect of your life. List them below:**

**Step 2: Now get centered and quiet. Take each separately and focus on how this "essence" feels as you state the following: "I am feeling _____." Allow the feeling of your chosen essence to wash over you, and truly FEEL it!**

**Step 3: Next, continue to FEEL the essence as you state: "I am full of _____." Feel the essence all around and inside of yourself. Enjoy the experience and get to really know this vibrational feeling that your essence brings to you.**

**Step 4: Finally, re-visit this exercise several times per day... it only takes less than a minute per essence, so focus on your full list – one by one. And, after you have experienced the results, share this exercise with your clients!**

# Step 4 – Client E-Valuation

In this chapter you'll find an exercise that will help you to guide your client in determining the focus of his/her subconscious mind to better understand what that person is energetically attracting. It will explain how the client consciously and subconsciously attracts both what he desires and also what he would like to avoid.[14]

## Part I:     E-Valuating from the Inside -- Out

In my opinion, whenever a person starts a new program or a new year or a new stage of life, it's important to know certain things before wasting time setting goals or jumping into the new program or the new stage.

***The things that one needs to ask him/herself to clarify are:***
- Who am I? - relates to values, beliefs, old habits, old patterns,
- What do I want? - they can't attract anything unless they are clear about this,
- What must I do to get what I want?

***There are two steps to this.***
1. The inner step is to identify one's internal values and align the energies so that they are not in internal conflict.
2. The outer step is the one we're most familiar with, which is setting the goals or taking action steps.

---

[14] For a more detailed version of this exercise including 2 hours of mp3 recording plus e-guide go to:
http://arielagroup.com/products/free_products.php .

**Evaluating What Your Client Chooses to ATTRACT into his/her life:**

*Ask your client to jot down ten emotions or values that he would like to have in his life to answer the following questions:*

- What is most important to me in life?
- What do I really want to feel in my life?
- What do I choose to attract into my life?

*Here are some values that you might suggest to your client:*

Abundant!
Active!
Alive sexually!
At Peace!
Aware!
Balanced!
Beautiful!
Bright!
Calm!
Clear!
Comfortable!
Compassionate!
Confident!
Connected!
Conscious!
Creative!
Empowered!
Energetically Expanded!
Energized!

Excited!
Exhilarated!
Expanded!
Flexible!
Free!
Full of Energy!
Full of Vitality!
Growing!
Having Fun!
Healthy & Vital!
In the Flow!
In tune!
Inspired!
Intuitive!
Joyful!
Light!
Loving/
Loved!
Needed &

Useful!
Open to Life!
Opportunity-ful!
Pain free!
Peaceful!
Plentiful!
Present!
Quiet!
Receptive!
Rejuvenated!
Resonant!
Resilient!
Resonating!
Safe!
Satiated!
Satisfied!
Secure!
Still!
Stimulated!
Etc

## Prioritizing your values into the order of importance

*Take the list of ten emotions/characteristics/values, and focusing on the first and second on the list, ask your client the following question:*

"Which feels more important to you: Number 1 or Number 2?"

*After she has made this decision, then take the new Number 1 and compare it to Number 3 asking:*

"Which feels more important to you: Number 1 or Number 3?"

*Take the highest item here (which becomes Number 1) and then compare it to Number 4 saying:*

"Which feels more important to you: Number 1 or Number 4?"

*Guide your client through this process with all of the ten items until you have identified a firm top priority Number 1.*

*Next, set aside the value Number 1 and follow this same process to identify the client's official Number 2 value.*

After you have supported your client to identify the exact priority of all ten (or more) values, then you both will know how she makes decisions and on what she bases her life decisions.

## What happens when values are set up for the wrong reasons?

So far in this section you have guided your client to identify the values, characteristics, situations, or feelings that he/she wants to attract into his life. Then you prioritized these.

There are times when people may have set values or intentions based on past experiences that didn't feel good. A client may have created a positive value, but it's based on negative experiences.

In order to get beyond that, you may need to guide your client in some energy work to clear out the old remnants and subconscious memory of the negative that caused him/her to want these particular positive values in her life. This is a good point at which to do some meridian tapping together and assign more personal work for the client to undertake between this and your next session.

## Part II:    Identifying Values or Conditions Your Client Wishes to Avoid

Now that you have helped your client to identify the positive values, it is a good next exercise to identify values or feelings that she wishes to AVOID at all risk because these can cause subconscious self-sabotage and worse.

**To start identifying the values, conditions, beliefs your client wishes to avoid, guide her to ask the following questions:**

- What is most important to avoid feeling in my life?
- What feelings do I really want to avoid?
- What patterns may be occurring in my life around these issues I'd like to avoid?

**Some examples of these "Negative Emotional Congruency Factors or Values" are:**

Shame

Insecurity

Humiliation

Boredom

Fear

Self loathing

Rejection

Frustration

Self-doubt

Hate

Guilt

Betrayal

Sadness

Anger

Disappointment

Deserted

Lost

Lacking

Resentment

Anger

Trauma

Terror

Grief

Loss

**Add more here:**

*Guide your client to list her own "Negative Values" or Emotional Conditions or Issues that she Wishes to Avoid:*

## Prioritizing Negative Emotional Factors

*Like you did with the positive values, now ask your client to rank these aspects that he/she wishes to avoid using the same exercise as the one used for ranking the positive values.*

*To place them in order have your client use one of the following statements:*

"I would rather avoid feeling __X__ than __Y__." (Compare the 1st & next on the list.)
"I work hardest to avoid feeling __X__ over feeling __Y__."

*Remember to take the highest or 1st on the client's list and compare it to each other item on the list. Then take the second highest on the list and compare it to each other item, and so on until you have every negative value ranked by importance.*

## Clearing the Charge that Attracts

The next step is to clear out the charge that your client may have on each of these negative emotional factors or values.

Start with the top value and personalize the following sequence.

# N-hanced EFT Tapping Sequence for Clearing Charge Around Negative Values

Personalize these sequences for your client by putting in appropriate words for his/her situation and tapping at the point indicated. For more information about WHERE to tap, please view the short video found at:
http://is.gd/EFTTappingPts

### *Karate Chop point:*

Even though I have a fear about attracting this in my life . . . I deeply and completely understand why I have this resistance.
On some level, I know why I am avoiding this feeling.
I know that my subconscious is protecting me from being hurt.
Even though I really want to avoid this in my life . . . and in the past this has felt really horrible to me . . . and the experience I had before was very uncomfortable to me . . . I really never want to feel this again.
I want to be free from this feeling or this situation.
I want just the opposite of this old feeling or condition.
I choose to live a wonderful life, completely free of this old condition, this old thing that I am avoiding.
I can let go of the memory of this.
I can let go of the fear of attracting this into my life.
I can let go of even thinking about the possibility of attracting this into my life.
I choose to be safe from this condition and this feeling.
I know that I protect myself as best I can.
I know that I can let go of the charge around feeling this way.
I know I can let go of the charge around attracting this into my life.
I know I can let go of all charge so I absolutely am not magnetizing this to myself.
I am letting it go now.

I am clearing it out of my system now
I am moving on and letting it go, from my past, this old fear.
I'm giving myself the freedom to move forward without this.

## Eyebrow point:

It makes me angry to think that I'm carrying this in my subconscious.
This is something that I really want to avoid.
I feel it's time now to completely clear it and let it go.
Worry only keeps it in my subconscious.
I can completely let it go now.
I can feel peacefulness and have it totally gone.

## Outer Eye point:

I am letting go of resentment about having this charge in my system.
I resent that I had a bad experience in the past about this.
I resent that I feel what I felt from bad past experiences.
I resent that I put too much energy already into avoiding this.
I resent that I have been held captive by this emotion, this fear, trying to avoid this.
I can let myself freely let it go now.
It no longer serves me to carry this around.
Thinking about it or worrying about it only gives it power.
The past is the past and I can let it go.
I'm ready to create a whole new scenario without this old issue or this old feeling.
I'm letting it go now.

## Under the Eye point:

I am claiming my personal power back now.
Trying to avoid this issue has just sucked my energy.
It hit me in the stomach, in the solar plexus.
It sapped my power and my energy.
It's caused me stress.

I choose to have peace of mind.
I choose to have clarity.
I choose to let this old feeling, the fear of this feeling, go right now.
I'm letting it go.

## Under the Nose point:

I really love myself.
I really respect myself.
I love my new visions for myself, my dreams and intentions for myself.
I feel so potent sometimes . . . and it's time now to let go totally of this thing I was trying to avoid.
It's absolutely time to let it out of my energy system completely now.
I can totally forget about it, let it go completely now.
I can be free to flow freely without being held back by any old things I'm trying to avoid.

## Chin point:

There have been times when I've been ashamed and embarrassed that I was so worried about this showing up in my life.
I've been embarrassed and ashamed when that old situation happened in my life that might have caused me to want to avoid it ever happening again.
I can let go of that.
I can hold my head up very proudly now.
I can go forward without fear.
I'm ready to go forward freely without anymore self-sabotaging.
It is time for me to feel good about moving forward in my life.
I'm letting go of any old beliefs that are holding me back.

## Collarbone point:

I have felt fear about this condition coming into my life for too long.
I have been afraid.
I have been avoiding this feeling in my life.
I have been afraid and I've been avoiding attracting this situation into my life.
It's time to let go of the fear.
I don't need the fear anymore.
Feeling afraid does not serve me; it only holds me back.
I'm letting go of all fear around this situation.
I can let it go for good now.
I can take off the charge and it won't be in my system anymore.
I'm ready, willing and able to let it go.
It's time to clear it out.

### Under the Arm point:

I have everything I need to be totally successful in my life.
I have everything I need to be happy and healthy and live a life of abundance.
I have everything I need to attract all the values I really want to have into my life.
Now is the time to let go of this issue that no longer serves me.
I'm ready, willing and able to let it go now.

### Top of Head point:

I'm grateful that I have these wonderful tools to use now.
I am grateful that my wonderful subconscious has protected me up to this point.
I am grateful that I have cleared the charge on this issue and I know how to continue clearing any little residue that's left.
And so it is.

# Other Values Issues to Consider With Your Client

As you guide your clients to go deeper, you must pay close attention to the many ways in which values can conflict and cause inner incongruencies and blockages that will result in self-sabotage, emotional and physical pain.

Positive Value  ← // → Positive Value
Positive Value ← // → Negative Value

### *It is important to become congruent with each of these:*

- Positive Values & their Priorities with each other and with your life
- Negative Values & their Priorities + Impacts on your life
- Positive Value versus Positive Value (conflicts)
- Positive Value versus Negative Value (conflicts)
- Negative Foundation under a Positive Value

### *Here are a number of related examples:*

- Positive Values & their Priorities

Example: Feeling that "being spiritual"( rather than "supporting my family well") needs to be #1 priority based on an old belief that spiritual people don't focus on making money.  [Guide your client to tap away charge on this issue so that no "should's" govern his values.]

- Negative Values & their Priorities

Example: "Never wanting to be fat like X." – and yet, hating diet & exercise. Underlying energy under the "never wanting to be..." attracts just that. [Help her tap away charge around both.]

- Positive Value versus Positive Value (conflicts)

Example: "Wanting to treat X number of clients." At the same time your client "Only wants to work 3 days per week." Maybe this doesn't seem possible in his belief system. [Tap away doubt.]

- Positive Value versus Negative Value (conflicts)

Example: Wanting to "Live like a rich person" versus "Hating certain greedy rich people" can cause inner conflict. [Tapping on all attitudes around rich people will help your client.]

- Negative Foundation under a Positive Value

Example: Memories of being poor haunt your client still so she sets a value of attracting a lifestyle of plenty. [Tapping is required here to dissolve the negative charge that is behind her positive value or desire.]

Example: Guilt about a bad relationship mistake leads to the creation of a value to attract the "perfect" relationship. Without tapping out the guilt and other issues around the failed relationship no new relationship will ever be near to "perfect". [Help your client tap through all aspects of the bad relationship that come to mind.]

# Step 5 – Personal Goal Identification

Identification of individual goals and how they can be achieved is the main focus of this section, and it can only be achieved if your client is in balance with where he/she has been, has focused on a personal vision, has identified both positive and resistance values, and has cleared a certain amount of inner resistance.

One of the primary aspects of goal setting in this form of Advanced or Transformative Coaching program is to ensure that the client identifies the **FEELINGS** that go along with the goal results. This is of paramount importance, and energetically is how your client will actually attract the achievement of each goal into his or her reality. This clarity of the difference between the inner and outer work involved with goal achievement provides the foundation for setting goals.

I like to remind clients that vibration is so much more dynamic in goal setting than left brain strategizing. When a person focuses on how it will feel when the goal is completed and he/she is living the results, then the rest of the details are secondary. When holding the vibration of the **FEELINGS** first, with an openness to move forward, the client is usually full of inspiration as to which steps relate to supporting the goal and will follow through without the normal resistance of putting this planning step first.

## Overview of the Goal Planning Process

It can be helpful to use a protocol as you move your client toward identifying and setting goals.
1. Set your session intentions.
2. Support your client to set practical and attainable Personal Goals .
3. Review specific client goals and place them individually within the context of the **Goal Planning**

**Exercise**.[15] It may be most beneficial to work through this exercise with your client rather than simply assigning it the first time. For subsequent goals after the first one the client should be able to carry out the process on his/her own.

4.  Remind your client about the INNER work that accompanies all OUTER actions, and guide him or her to FEEL the results so he/she can set the process in motion.
5.  Help the client clear inner blockages as they come up.
6.  Remember and Point out that your client is complete and right wherever s/he is supposed to be.
7.  Focus on your client's needs, goals, agenda, values.
8.  De-Brief your client around Personal Goals using the **Goal Planning Exercise** after working on the first goal and all subsequent individual goals.
9.  Identify where your client is NOW... and discuss the Critical Gap between here and  where your client chooses to be for each goal.
10. Guide your client to see how to get the desired results by revisiting the Multi-sensory Vision, Values, focus on FEELINGS, and finally by setting action steps and carrying them out in an organized and supported plan.

## Setting Personal Goals

As you and your client prepare for and take time to complete and review the **Goal Planning Exercise**[16] as well as the **Multisensory Vision**[17] , you can start to fine-tune the planning process.

Your client has more than one goal in mind, so for EACH goal

---

[15] See **Appendix 7**
[16] See **Appendix 7**
[17] See **Appendix 5**

a separate **Goal Planning Exercise** should be created. Based on this, you and your client can identify the priority of goals, placing the first one as top priority and identifying subsequent goals (that will either take care of themselves as the earlier priority goals are achieved, or that must be scheduled in next priority order.)

Looking at your coaching schedule, you and your client can start to identify how much time each goal warrants and sketch out a plan with projected goal achievement dates. (Remember that these can shift in either direction; they are merely a guide for keeping your client on task and helping him/her to experience the continuity of the coaching program.)

## Setting the Coaching Tone

Not only have you as a coach been taught how to be "in tune" with your client, but you can support your client's success by sharing three key attributes that he/she must accept in him/herself and others in order for success to occur.

*The client is complete NOW.* If your client accepts that he/she is complete, then they take on a stronger, more powerful energy and are more ready to move forward toward achieving personal goals.

*The client is right where he/she is supposed to be and will progress according to his/her own pace.* When your client believes this, then unnecessary pressure is removed and there is freedom to flow forward in a more natural manner. This imbues the process with a sense of surrender to the bigger powers, and with that comes a greater sense of ease as the goal is approached.

It is all about the client's needs, goals, agenda, and values as he/she identifies the baseline, the goals, and the most practical action steps. As their coach you must support your clients in the best ways possible for each particular client. Flexibility, with focus on your client's needs, goals, agenda, values will support you and your client to co-create the most beneficial working relationship for success.

## De-briefing around Personal Goals

In order for you to best support your client to move forward and achieve his/her goals, it is necessary for you to be able to customize your coaching approach and your client's own awareness to the issues of:

- The habits and patterns that indicate where a client is.
- The habits and patterns that keep a client stranded or stuck.
- The habits and patterns that move the client forward.

# Step 6 – Being Present & Centered

Look over the following sample script and customize a comfortable way for you to introduce to your client the concept of being present.

*" I am glad to be back with you for your coaching session. My intention is that as we begin to work on your goals in a powerful and centered way, we will work on some concepts that will support you to successfully achieve them. We will review these in today's session."*

Let your client share his/her intention now.

*"Today I want to share a part of the coaching that you hired me for.*

 The concept is about being fully present in order to empower the client.

*When I am here with you right now, I am not listening to other things that are going on; I am listening to you.*

 The concept of being fully present is one that you will want to use more and more in your own life... to enable you to be conscious in your life as well as present and conscious with others around you.

This is the ability to hear in a conscious way where you are 100% committed to a conversation.

## Four Steps to Being Fully Present:

In order for your client to be successful in achieving his or her goals he/she must learn to be fully present and conscious with him/herself and others.

In this coaching step you can walk your client through the process of understanding how to be present by discussing the four characteristics necessary in order to do this.

1. Releasing EGO blockages.
2. Recognizing and speaking personal TRUTH.
3. Recognizing and releasing ATTACHMENT.
4. Becoming aware of personal patterns, habits, beliefs and releasing JUDGMENT.

## Getting Centered

There is value in having some kind of centering that says we're together, focused in the present moment, not multi-tasking.

It is very important that you have the basic structure for bringing your client in and helping to quiet his/her mind in a centered way so that your session can be more profound. Often coaches miss this element and the coaching session cannot go as deeply into real issues of the moment, so the coaching opportunity is missed.

You must create a format that is replicable and models consistency to your clients. In your centering process create a safe place where you and your client share your intentions. Intentions can be very simple, and the important thing is to be in the moment where they rise to the surface and can be shared in a powerful way.

## Practical Applications for YOU:
Rate yourself at the end of each coaching session during a week to determine to what extent you have adopted this in your own life and coaching practice.

1- Absent -2---------3-Fully-Present-4---------5-Sometimes-Present-6---------7-Un-focused-8---------9- Fully Present -10

# Step 7 – Organizing the Client

## Pre-Coaching Form[18]

This is a form that you co-create with your client. You agree to receive it 24 hours before each coaching session. Your clients can fax or e-mail it to you with their input for the session.

In the form you can collect the evidences of positive shifts as they occur for your client. The form will also include your client's intention for the next session, and what they want to feel and accomplish. It should include what is working and what is going right that they are celebrating.

The form should also list what things are not quite right yet and some of the challenge areas where there is a gap between NOW and your client's VISION. They should be able to report to you what they noticed this week that showed up in their life, what's working, what resources have appeared, what people have shown up, etc.

The form should provide an opportunity for your client to very clearly focus on what they want to gain in this next session. If your client shows up and hasn't really thought about this next session, you fall into the model of coaching that doesn't work or that steals too much discovery time from each session.

Have your client look at his/her goals and identify what actions they've accomplished since the last session. What are the items that you and the client co-created together and decided were your priorities? What did you do with them?

---

[18] Use **Appendix 4** as a guide to developing a customized Pre-coaching form with your client.

# Post-Coaching Report Form[19]

This form can be co-created so that the impact of the coaching session is reinforced. Often clients (and coaches too) spend much of their focus during a session in the process of taking notes. A post-coaching report form allows your client to be organized and it affords the opportunity to review notes and go more deeply into the content of the session while it is still fresh in the client's mind.

This form can be designed to contain the different topics discussed on the call, with what actions the client is going to take, what lessons were learned in the session, or what shifts occurred for your client during the session. In essence, the form can include all that your client learned in the coaching session.

Another important item to be included on this form is what coaching skill was covered on the call. Remember that you are activating coaching skills in your client, so a re-statement and review of their new coaching skill is an important element to include in the post-coaching review.

The form can also include what your clients are learning about themselves and what decisions they are making.

Another self-motivator on the form may be a list of what the client's next three steps are. This becomes a review of plan and direction as well as a written commitment to three action goals.

Remember that the entire intention behind this form is to help your clients be very much focused and be more intentional so that they achieve what they want.

---

[19] Go to **Appendix 4** and use the sample there to co-create a usable Post-coaching form with each of your clients.

## Co-creating the Forms

Co-create the two forms with your clients; give them some suggestions and have them put the forms together.

Ask your clients what would be helpful for them to have on their forms. You can call the forms anything you want.

Just remember that it is beneficial to you as a coach to receive information ahead of your coaching session that will give you a snapshot of what's been happening with your client and what actions they want to focus in on. Also, a follow-up form allows you and your client to both better understand the content, impact, and significance of the coaching session.

## Practical Applications for YOU:

Review **Appendix 4** to create sample forms with which you personally resonate. Then you can share these with your clients in order to co-create the best usable forms for the duration of your coaching experience with each individual.

# Step 8 – Self-Coaching Techniques

You have already spent time teaching your client to use EFT and other energy therapy tools on their own. You've done this by modeling their use as well as specifically guiding clients through the processes and instructing them to do each step skillfully.

In this section you will learn three additional "tools" that will empower your client to move beyond needing to rely on a practitioner for coaching. This will not cost you your clients, however it will provide your clients with powerful tools that they will be able to use for the rest of their lives, with or without your help.

The Self-coaching tools that we will cover here are the following:
- Asking Powerful Questions
- Making Powerful Observations
- Making Powerful Requests

## Introduction to Powerful Questions

Expert coaching includes LISTENING and ALLOWING your client to be creative in how he or she shares. In order to best facilitate this process it is beneficial to understand how to create POWERFUL QUESTIONS that will inspire your clients to really TUNE IN more deeply and that will elicit the most effective communication from your client.

Although as a coach you can plan some very helpful questions ahead, the POWERFUL questions come from the moment, and are more intuitive. It is also imperative that you know WHEN to interject POWERFUL questions in your conversations with clients in your coaching sessions.

### There should be a PURPOSE for using POWERFUL QUESTIONS:

- to help your client look at a situation differently,
- to help your client clarify something about the situation,
- to help your client move faster to take specific action.

POWERFUL questions are used to ACTIVATE your client, and you will be more effective in this area if you are guided by your own intuition. This should not be difficult for you as an energy therapist because intuition drives your sessions more than traditional non-energy therapist coaches.

It is best for you to know HOW to create powerful questions, and to create them on the spot when most appropriate. The focus here is to help you and your client to find your client's TRUTH. Powerful Questions can go to the depth necessary to reach and bring forth this TRUTH.

Also, remember that this process guides you to teach your clients to coach themselves, so it is important to activate their coaching skills as you model for them. Not only will you support powerful coaching sessions with the Questions that you ask, but you will be activating the ability to coach in your clients.

## How to Create Powerful Questions

Below is a check-list of HOW to prepare to ask POWERFUL QUESTIONS:

1. Fully tune in to your client at a deep, intuitive level. BE THERE – LISTEN!! Let your intuition take over. TRUST the process and focus on your client.
2. Listen and HEAR deeply to recognize the tone, emotion,

behavior patterns, strengths, what is said, and what lies underneath what is said.

3. Be fully ready for your client's response to your POWERFUL question, and be detached from the outcome so that you have no agenda about the answer.

4. BE in the moment of the coaching session – WITH your client, and just let questions flow directly from your intuition.

## Characteristics of Powerful Questions

A Powerful Question is:

- Always in response to the client.
- Always has a coaching purpose.
- Is present oriented with future implications.
- Makes the client stop.
- Helps the client tell their truth more quickly.
- Helps a client separate facts from interpretation.
- Can be uncomfortable for the coach and/or the client.
- Is asked simply, in the client's language, and reflects one issue.
- Elicits an answer, forward movement, and concordant energy and action.

Activating the use of POWERFUL QUESTIONS within your coaching practice and in your clients is a very potent process!! As we utilize the process with clients, then we also activate the client to use the process for him/herself too.

Don't pre-plan questions – just BE THERE and BE a coach with a tool that can be easily utilized: that of asking POWERFUL questions.

As you help your client to activate the skill of asking Powerful Questions you are providing a strong service, just as you do in supporting him or her to expertly learn to use EFT or other energy therapy tools in their lives. To ask oneself specific deep and Powerful questions can be very powerful.

And, next is to learn to step back and Observe.

## Making Powerful Observations

This is an important skill that you will activate in your coaching clients for their empowered use in self-coaching. It is an advanced coaching technique, and before utilizing it your client must realize that in order to make a Powerful Observation he must:

- Be "in tune" with the person with whom they are working,
- Participate in a natural, normal conversation,
- Implement deep listening as they are tuned into the other person,
- Hold what is most useful for the other person as paramount in importance,
- Feel for the "opening" where a coaching observation can be inserted.

The purpose of a Powerful Observation is to help your client move forward and/or to shift the energy. As you utilize this technique you and your client will notice its impact. You may wish to point out some of the key points of creating and utilizing Powerful Observations to your client. And, as in other techniques, tapping along never hurts... and can assist in the learning process too.

You must be prepared for whatever response to your Powerful Observation comment may come. The person being observed and coached will simply respond with his/her TRUTH, so it will come from that person and the observer should be open to any response without arguing, rebutting, or taking it personally. [This is an important tool that must be activated in you as an energy therapist and coach first, as there is nothing more disempowered than a therapist or coach who has had his/her "buttons pushed".]

The best Powerful Observations come when they are appropriate and when there is an opportunity for the client to move forward. These statements of observation show a level of CARING on the part of the observer or coach.

## Characteristics of Powerful Observations

A powerful observation is:

- Always truthful.
- Not about the coach being right.
- Told without charge or judgment, and never places the client in the wrong.
- Will often enhance the client's focus on issues and awareness of where he or she is within the "critical gap".
- Provides a strong foundation for the client to grow, change, and move forward.

In the discipline of using energy therapies and EFT you are probably already observing your clients for energy shifts, reactions, emotional shifts, additional emotional impacts, so for you this section may simply be an analysis of what you already do.

For your clients the points covered in this section may support them to create better relationships, learn to speak their TRUTH, and be better equipped to observe both themselves and others in order to better understand.

After you have modeled and taught the use of Powerful Questions and Observation, it is now appropriate for you to focus on Making Powerful Requests of your clients in order to support their growth and accountability.

## Powerful Requests

This is another energy-shifting tool, and in order to make a Powerful Request you must:
- Be in tune with your client.
- Hear deeply.
- Be ready to respond to your client.
- Think big.
- Be ready for your client's response.

## Characteristics of the Powerful Request

A Powerful Request:
- When acted upon, will help your client to close or narrow a critical gap.
- Is always bigger than where the client is today, and, if acted upon, will move the client forward in his or her goals.
- Often creates possibilities.
- Gets the client to believe in and trust who they are.
- May lighten the client.

Remember to walk your client through these characteristics so that he/she may then utilize the tool with greater understanding.

## Advanced Coaching Assignment

The only way that you will be able to teach your client about the Advanced Coaching tools discussed in this section is to use and teach these techniques in a guided sequence so that your client may experience and participate in the process. As appropriate you may dissect each step for further clarification and personal self-coaching use. At the beginning, however, experiencing the processes is most beneficial.

### Follow these coaching steps:

1. Implement an Advanced Coaching session with your client that includes a focus on the issues and goals of the moment and the utilization of Powerful Questions, Observations, and Requests.
2. Discuss Powerful Questions, Observations, Requests with your client for his/her better understanding.
3. Amp up the power of the coaching experience by incorporating these techniques into your sessions with your client and urging your client to utilize them in self-coaching.


4. Guide your client to record his/her usage of the new tools in the pre-coaching sheets for subsequent coaching sessions. (You might want to co-create with your client some adaptations to the Pre-Coaching Form at this time.)[20]

## Points to Consider about Questions, Observations, Requests

As a coach it is good for you to think "bigger" than others (in order to best serve your client.) You can do this when you use POWERFUL QUESTIONS, OBSERVATIONS, and REQUESTS.

We don't see ourselves truly:  we see a reflection of ourselves. We really want to see ourselves (and help our clients see themselves) as higher, bigger, with a higher vibration, so more powerful tools are necessary to shift energy and amp up positive movement.

See your clients as they WANT TO BE - NOT as they are with

---

[20] Go to **Appendix 4**

their weaknesses. Don't hold them back - see them as PERFECT NOW and show up with that activated in you. If you see their downfalls, then that is what you reflect to the client and they will show up in that light.

## In your Advanced Coaching, remember:

Clients are always as they desire to be!!! You will attract and see in your client what you perceive in your client. You must hold a positive expectation in order to activate the positive results in your client. You help clients (and then they help themselves and others) to shift by seeing something different - and that may be the perception of success. Watch your self-talk – it must be positive!!! Activate this for yourself and your clients!!

# Step 9 – Self Empowerment Skills

The goal of most successful coaches is taking your client to a point and then helping him or her to continue progressing forward. When this happens your client gets to better know himself and his life view becomes more positive.

The goal of most successful energy therapists is to continue to support the clearing of all blockages in your client so that she may more easily flow forward, identify when her progress is impeded and support her to clear obstacles, and generally to help her to create a more positive life.

This section will provide coaching skills to further develop your client's ability to empower and to grow himself or herself, taking life to the next level.

## Tips to GROW Your SELF or Someone Else:  From the Inside-Out

The following tips are beneficial to you as a coach as well as your client. And, these will allow your client to support herself as well as others.

### As you coach, focus on these inner steps:

- Be in the now…. Be present.
- The first step is to identify and change all self-talk to positive.
- Look for just the good in life… don't dwell on the negative. (Remember: you attract that upon which you focus your attention!)
- Look at all details… and focus on just the positive ones.
- Focus on what is WORKING!!!
- What are the universal "essences" that you want to

create in your life?[21]

- Appreciate – even if it is something small to appreciate.
- What is the next "inspired" action for you to take??
- Identify and flow with your natural strengths.
- What are your natural brilliances??
- What are tasks you can enjoy doing??
- What are actions you can take that support your inner "essences".
- Believe in yourself… and believe in OTHERS!!
- Notice the difference in the statements below… and never state definitely a negative about yourself or another
  - X seems to be a procrastinator. OR X really wants to move forward.
  - X seems reluctant to change. OR X truly wants to change her life.
  - X seems to be depressed. OR X really wants to be happy.
- Communicate that you believe in yourself and others (Hold the vision for others.)
- Note that even small children really have the solutions to problems
- Affirmations are potent only when they have positive emotion behind them!!
- Take very small action steps… don't claim to be a millionaire if you can't pay your rent yet.
- Use progressive affirmations that are more positive than old patterns.
- Keep creating affirmations until your inner voice has no resistance… and tap as you go.
- Bring each affirmation to a point where you believe it using EFT and other energy medicine techniques. You may work up to it gradually:
  - "Maybe someday I will be able to manage plenty of money in my life."
  - "Someday I will have plenty of money in my life,

---

[21] Refer back to *Step 3* for the *Vibrational Essence Exercise*.

and I will be able to manage it."
  - o "Someday soon I will have plenty of money in my life and will be willing and able to manage it."
  - o "Soon I will have plenty of money in my life and it will be FUN to manage it!"
  - o "I am feeling the money in my life now."
  - o "I am witnessing the money flowing into my life now!"
  - o "I am totally enjoying the process of attracting, having, and using money in my life!"
  - o Etc.
- Amp up your positive language... shift your self-talk and how you address others to include only a focus on positive!!
- Use a "wrist rubber band exercise" where you "twang" your wrist each time that you think or speak something negative... just as a reminder until you purge negativity from your inner self.

## Four Question Framework for Inner Work:

In the book *Loving What Is,* the author, Byron Katie, describes her profound technique of re-connecting with the collective consciousness called "The Work".[22] Her process includes the use of Four seemingly simple questions, but questions that can alter your inner perspective or perception... which ultimately is your reality.

I highly recommend reading her book, as it guides you through the full process and it application in a number of case studies. She first assigns a Worksheet that guides a client to log in feelings (usually with blame for them pointed to another person), and then uses the questioning process to help the clients understand and unravel the specific problems in their

---

[22] Katie, Byron (Byron Kathleen Mitchell); with Stephen Mitchell. (2002) *Loving What Is: Four Questions That Can Change Your Life.* NY, NY: Three Rivers Press/ Random House, Inc.

lives. By reading the book you will best understand how to apply the questions and then to flip the focus from the other person to you  for optimal outcomes.

**Here are the Four Questions to ask _yourself_ as you focus on a thought that bothers you,... and then use it with your client:**

1- Is it true?
2- Can you absolutely know that it is true?... or is this just your fear?
3- How do you react when you think that thought?... emotions and behavior?
4- Who would you be without the thought?... & your reactions to it?

Disclaimer:  In simply asking the previous questions you are not really applying "The Work", however, this simple part of the process can still shed some light on a faulty perception, and can lead to some inner shifts around unbeneficial thoughts.

## BUILDING Your SELF and Others:

Building yourself is done a bit more on the OUTER, and yet, it is similar to Growing yourself. Here are some tips and questions to ask yourself:

- Create a firm foundation using the same techniques as Growing Your SELF and Others.
    - Focus on getting better and better, and growing yourself from the inside-outward.
    - Know how you and your clients can grow and build up yourselves... and others.
    - Be a coach more than a boss.
    - Be a coach more than a parent.
    - Be a coach in all appropriate areas of your life.

- Identify your intentions: What do you want/choose?? – How is it supposed to FEEL??
- What essence(s) or feelings do you choose to have in all aspects of your life??
- Take and support the steps in goal-setting and goal-attainment:
    - Support the resolve/persistence to reach the goal... and tap away all resistance.
    - Know clearly what your goal is... or tap until you reach clarity.
    - Be open to the inspired actions that you will take each day to move forward toward the goal... keep yourself clear to receive the inspiration.
- Remind yourself daily of WHY you choose to, and HOW you can reach the goal.
- Re-adjust your goals... amp them up to BIGGER and FASTER results!!
- Make extreme requests of yourself... and others.
- CHANGE your behavior in order to get different/bigger and faster results!! Do it differently this time!!... this time add energy therapy to boost the efficiency of your process as well as speed the response time.
- MODEL IT!! MODEL your goal... and how you will/DO feel with the results.

## Five Question Framework for Outer Work:

In the book *Breaking the Rules*[23] the author illustrates in simple terms why we need to move our focus from what is not working or why it has not worked, to what IS working. He explains why when we are in that place of focusing on what is not working we literally cannot access the part of our brains that has solutions for us!

---

[23] Wright, Kurt. *Breaking the Rules: Removing the Obstacles to Effortless High Performance*. (1998) Boise, ID: CPM Publications.

Our society teaches us to be critical and to look at what is NOT working. This becomes automatic sabotage for anything we wish to accomplish or manifest in our lives.

To help us re-train our thinking *Breaking the Rules* introduces a mental exercise entitled **The Five Question Framework**. This supports anyone using it to shift the mental energetics and focus more on the positive, higher vibrational thought processes that lead to success.

This is a potent technique to guide a very short coaching or self-coaching session.

### Just ask the following five questions:

1. What IS working??
2. What makes that work?? – Why is it right??
3. What is the IDEAL VISION of your life/business/finances/relationship/ etc.??
4. What is NOT QUITE RIGHT YET??
5. What resources can you use to improve the situation NOW??

## Self Building and Guiding Worksheet:

Your client must moderate his/her own self-talk!  One way to do this is to guide your client to identify... daily (or even more frequently)... the positive aspects that ARE working in his/her life, relationships, business, etc. The following short exercise can amp up your client's energetic vibration:

What **IS WORKING** for you today??

*List below all that you can think of now using the following categories as a guide:*

- Personal Life:


- Health and Well-being:


- Relationships:


- Professional Life/ Business:


- Finances:


- Other:

# Step 10 – Managing Goals

With the new awareness and empowerment your client now is ready to review and manage his or her goals. At this stage he can better clarify, focus, accelerate the goal, or change it altogether.

## Goal Setting Patterns

As a coach you need to understand human nature as it relates to accomplishing goals, and as an energy therapist you already understand blockage patterns, inherited issues, and detrimental issues related to emotional trauma – all that can negatively affect the setting of and attainment of goals.

Often clients are so set in past habits and systems that even though they might set a worthy goal, getting started is a very difficult step. Human nature or environmental "nurture" often sets a block when any kind of behavior change is concerned, so even with a set goal, it takes extra committed energy (and often YOUR assistance as a coach/ energy therapist) to move forward to take even the first step toward achieving the client's goal.

Then, even after some momentum is gained, there may be a lull where your client gets tired, confused, "stuck", and will again need your assistance to help move back into this newly created "groove" and maintain and gain more momentum toward achieving the goal.

### *Common patterns around self-sabotaging one's goals are:*

1- Don't even know where to start... shifting priorities... timing for start doesn't work into habits/ on-going schedule...
2- Start was OK... lost momentum after awhile... tired and

confused...

3- Moved forward easily from start... getting close to goal... hit the wall / everything fell apart...,

4- Or, moved right up to the goal without any struggle and then consciously stopped cold just before taking the final step to success... and couldn't budge another inch forward.

Your task here is to guide your client to activate and clear him/herself in order to understand and model the situation around setting goals, and better meet the goal(s).

It is very important to identify what IS WORKING. This will re-charge your client's energy and then help that person identify where they are in order to re-start and move forward toward the goal. This may also be an opportunity for your client to change their goal so that the newly identified goal will hold more passion and support the motivation in the client to work on it.

And, it is equally important to identify exactly WHEN the process stopped and what your client felt at that point. Is there an old pattern, old habit, reminder of a past trauma, a fear of moving to that next step based on... ?  Only after identifying and clearing a potential emotional block can your client move on to complete or accelerate his or her goal.

## The Accelerated Goal

Your client may want to accelerate achieving the goal... to get results more quickly!!

It is important to understand and identify WHY the goal must be achieved more quickly. With this understanding, and getting it stated clearly, often there is automatic self-motivation involved. Guide your client to tap into the inner energy and passion behind activating the goal. That will assist in the momentum.

And, if the client is already intent on moving forward more quickly you can make sure he or she has no inner resistance to changing the time parameters, expecting sooner results, changing some action steps or the process itself, or simply focusing on the goal in a new way.

### It is critical that you support your client to:

- Know what she needs to do in order to best use time and energy toward meeting her goal, and
- Clear as she goes so that no inner resistance impedes her progress.

What are some specific interim goals that can be identified and reached on the way to achieving the final goal?? Your client must identify the support needed... and when it is needed.

And, as a coach, remember that YOU must be activating your own goals... and taking the same steps to accelerate the momentum in order to model it. It is important that you understand and apply the process in order to support your client in doing it. When you understand the experience you have had in your own life, then you can empower and guide your client with understanding behind your support.

Establish someone to hold you accountable... and identify if you are the one who will hold your client accountable... and who else will help.

In executing the plan, you must know what the next steps are that need to be accomplished. Self-coach yourself and guide your client in this process. You can create a roadmap for the goal and the interim goals.

Remember to guide your clients in each step of how to be

their own SELF Coach. It is a major part of coaching to instill in your client HOW to coach him/herself. This provides more value to your client and helps him to help others... and it often builds loyalty so that even though your client may become self-sufficient in many self-coaching ways, he will still find benefit in his association with you as you continue to guide him to reach even bigger goals.

Help your clients learn from their "contrasts" or challenges, so that they can continue to move forward without getting stuck or losing sight of their goals. A contrast or challenge often indicates that something new wants to be born, so these points can be seen as positive sign-posts along the journey toward reaching one's goals.

Remember to go back to the personal essences and values so that the goals can be set most effectively and the action steps will be identified based on what will support those desired feelings. This will allow the most effective actions to be taken and less time wasted on "busy work" actions that don't always support the chosen inner vibration.

## The Focused Plan

Having a focused plan ensures that your client is working on the one main goal... and this will take care of resolving other issues and accomplishing other minor goals. This helps keep you and your clients from becoming overwhelmed with too many goals all screaming at once to be accomplished.

Another way of looking at this from the perspective of an energy therapist is in the approach taken and shared by Gary Craig, creator of EFT/ Emotional Freedom Techniques. Gary insists that in clearing inner blocks you should focus on the biggest block or the one with most charge first. He compares this with a large tree in a forest that you wish to clear. By taking out the biggest tree first, when it falls it will automatically take out many smaller trees in its path, thus getting you broader results without as much effort. So, in clearing the biggest emotional issue, the smaller related issues are often cleared automatically. And, when you focus on your main goal, it often includes or cancels out many of the smaller goals that might be bogging down the process in the beginning.

**With this in mind, here are some tips to better focus YOUR plan... and then share the process with your clients:**

- Focous on ONE GOAL:
- Does this goal feel that it is MOST important??
- Temporarily agree to set other goals aside in order to focus on this one goal.
- Use the **Personal Goal Planning Exercise**[24] to create a master plan of action for each goal - one goal at a time.
- Coach yourself to maintain momentum on just ONE goal... don't drift away to another goal.
- Clear any inner emotional resistance that comes up... as it appears.
- Create a system to measure progress on that ONE goal. Establish consistent intervals to look at the goal and your progress.

By supporting your SELF and then your client to focus on ONE goal... and achieve it, this instills a sense of confidence in yourself and a deep level of loyalty between your client and you.

When a person achieves a BIG goal, then everything else shifts in that person's life. In the case of you helping your client to do this, when she accomplishes her goal and feels the resulting shifts she then may well feel a continued need

---

[24] See **Appendix 7**

for you to coach and support her on another goal. She may especially appreciate the momentum reached in achieving goals when you support her to win... and... this keeps her loyal to you and your coaching/ energy therapy process.

## Changing a Goal

You must support clients to feel free to adjust or change their goals if they seem unattainable or impractical. Goals don't need to be written in stone... they can evolve with the person, and they SHOULD do this. In order to be clear about when this is necessary, it is good to measure results periodically.

- When your client just doesn't find any energy or excitement around a goal, then maybe it is not a practical one to begin with, or maybe there is inner resistance present.
- If they are making progress, and are very stressed about this, then it may be a good idea to shift this goal or at least pause until the inner stress is cleared.
- If your client loses commitment, then it may be time to change the goal or determine and clear a blockage. Sometimes this goal is simply no longer important.
- If resources seem to be disappearing, so there is less support now than before, then check your client for inner blocks that may be causing an energy drain or at the least, a lack of focus. Sometimes, beyond clearing energetic blocks, it may also be beneficial to replace the resources or shift the goals.
- Sometimes it is all right to abandon the goal altogether. Lives shift, people evolve, interests shift, goals often lose their value. It is best to abandon a goal only after it has truly been focused on, knowing that there is no inner resistance, and its value has been determined to no longer exist practically for your client.

Remember to guide your client to update the **Personal Goal**

**Setting Exercise**[25] by periodically going back and reading it to shift any data that has changed and adjust goals that may no longer be practical.

There is no such thing in goal-setting as FAILURE. If the process and system are set up appropriately, then there is no chance for failure. Evolution will be measured and goals will be adjusted as you guide your client to create the new life that most speaks to his/her essences.

When you help them to gain momentum, they don't even consider that failure is an option. They know they can rely on you to guide them to stay on target, to focus, and to be successful as they adjust and focus and plan for transformation.

**Keeping Your "Finger on the Pulse" for Progress:**

Review notes for your client(s) and ensure that they are using their Pre- and Post-coaching sheets to communicate their successes and shifted goals as your coaching series with them continues.

---

[25] See **Appendix 7** for a reminder.

# Step 11 – The Benefits of PLAY!

When you guide your client to raise his/her vibration, many exciting opportunities will come to him/her. Coach your clients to activate the following skill-sets for many positive results.

## Recapturing PLAY in Life

You can share the following information directly with your client as you introduce the theme of this coaching session:

- Play is a lubricant in all aspects of life. In order to most easily FLOW through the details of life, PLAY is an important component. The energy of PLAY lifts one's spirits and the spirits of those around them. The frequency of PLAY is light and high, and attracts positive outcomes and ease of life details.

- Remember as a coach and energy therapist that YOU must activate PLAY in YOUR life in order to support that in your client. You must MODEL it and know the experience of the skill set in order to amp up the skills in your clients. And, they, in turn, must activate it in order to share it.

- Play raises your vibration to that of JOY. In this frequency the outcomes of even a stressful situation can be minimized and miracles can happen in front of your eyes.

- Play helps your client to tap into his/her passion and creativity. The more fun he has, the more easily his brain will flow from both the creative and analytical sides, without being blocked. Business meetings, strategizing sessions, serious issues can be handled most easily when PLAY is involved. Life can be FUN... and still very productive!!

## Activating PLAY in your Client

### *Ask your client:*

- What did you do during your childhood that gave you great JOY???
- What were playful activities that you enjoyed doing??
- How did you have FUN as a child??
- What are some ways you can introduce play into your life NOW on a DAILY basis?

### *Make the following suggestions to your client to add to her own list:*

- Go to a playground and watch kids play.
- Visit a park and watch children and families.
- Visit a toy store.
- Buy and play with balloons or water balloons.
- Buy a "magic wand" or "crystal ball" and play with it.
- Read a fun children's book.
- Visit the children's section of a bookstore, and just browse.
- Choose a fun activity from your own childhood, and re-live it – do it now!!
- Find a swing and USE IT!!
- Put on skits with your kids – put on a show.
- Finger paint, draw, have fun being artistic.

## New Ways to think about "WORK"

Guide your client to re-frame how she thinks about "WORK". If the word instills negative or heavy feelings, then coach her to create a new word to refer to what she does for pay. Some people talk about "playing at their J.O.B." Others re-name the process from "WORK" to "PLORK" (play+work).

When your client uses her imagination she lightens her

vibration. Also, in being creative and imaginative, her dreams begin the manifestation process.

Guide your clients to PLAY imaginary games even in "work" situations. The energy of imagining is similar to play and is of a higher vibration. This allows for exciting things to happen.

## Coach your SELF and your Client

In your own past how have you used your imagination that was fun and productive?

*Try the following to awaken your imagination:*

- Use crayons, paints, clay, etc. to create/draw your vision.
- Create a "visioning board" or collage to activate your subconscious.
- Create an on-going story with friends... take turns adding onto the story around a theme.
- Tell stories out loud or imagine stories about people you see around you.
- Be as silly and playful as possible... and use your imagination.
- Dress up and play different roles that appeal to you.
- Write a story about yourself where you are the key character... imagine exciting details and roles that you have always wanted to play.
- Imagine that negative aspects of life or "work" around you are only parts of a movie/video. Imagine the people as role actors – see specific movie stars playing their roles. See the situation as one of make-believe... this will lighten the load.

Only when you become more accustomed to PLAY in your own life can you activate it in your clients!

## Let go of Control!!

When life is being controlled, freedom is lost. Without introducing any danger, it is important for adults (especially) to let go of control. Coach your clients to be adventurous and spontaneous. Suggest that they enlist some friends to come with them and do some un-planned, fun activities on the spur of the moment. Child-like spontaneity will help them shift their energy and will raise the vibration of the situation.

When one lets go of control, then they expand their ability and range of trust. They loosen up the grip and ALLOW. They do not HAVE TO DO IT ALL when they let go of control. They attract support and allow things to happen around them that will save time, energy, and money.

Often people are forced to learn to let go of control. We all know people who have succumbed to personal tragedy or illness with the lesson or result being that they let go of control in their lives like never before. It is much easier if you support your clients to let go on their own – little by little – instead of waiting for life to force them to let go. Life will be easier and goals will be achieved more easily when control is released and play is activated.

Your goal is to help your client to discover things they may have lost. You want them to discover a place of lightness that they might not have experienced since they were children. You can help your clients make small shifts that are life changing and will support them to find ease and fun in all aspects of their lives.

You activate play and fun in your own life. Then you activate it in your clients. Then you guide them to activate play in their lives and in people around them. Can you imagine the excitement of going into "work" settings where joy and fun are the environmental tones for being productive??

## Play Activation Exercise

You can use the short exercise below with your clients to help them activate more PLAY in their lives:

*What is <u>one thing</u> NOW that you can do to incorporate more PLAY into your life... starting today??*

*What is one thing that can let you release control and be a bit more spontaneous in your life??*

*What are action steps that will help you to activate the above two things NOW??*

# Step 12 – Embracing Change

Change is a constant part of life!!

Coaches regularly help individuals and organizations CHANGE!!... it is in the nature of coaching.

There is a specific CHANGE CYCLE or PROCESS OF CHANGE, and one must understand this in order to get through it gracefully without pain. Anticipating the different aspects of change will support people to move forward with momentum. People can reap the rewards of change if they understand it better, so your job as a coach is to help your clients understand the change as you guide them through it. And, your role as an energy therapist is to help to remove all resistance and fear around change so that it can be enjoyed as a natural process instead of a trauma.

In order to flow forward in one's life, change must be a comrade that is well understood and appreciated for what it is. This section will set an important foundation for future sessions in your coaching of clients and in their self-coaching. If you understand change and help to model and define it for your clients as you guide them through their own changes, then you will become a pillar of support for them and can help them to move through additional levels of transformation.

## WHAT DRIVES CHANGE-The Change Motivators

Here are some of the more common catalysts or motivators for change with questions you may ask yourself or your client in order to distinguish each:

### Reactionary Change:
- Is the change a reaction to a shock or trauma??
- Is there a catalyst that helps somebody shift into change mode??

### Anticipatory Change:
- Is your client starting the change cycle because of something he is anticipating??
- A possible lay-off, divorce, etc.??
- Possibly pregnant or just diagnosed with something?? Others.

### Change From An Unknown Motivation:
- Following intuitive instincts to move toward change.
- An intuitive drive to change something is strong enough to activate it.
- The soul is calling...

### Change Due To Something Being "Not Quite Right":
- Wanting to make something even better.
- Following the feeling that life will be even better when something is changed.

## AREAS OF CHANGE

When I work with a client I often help him or her with change.

Some come to me for pro-active "Conscious Transformation" change where they know they want or need to make some deep changes, and ask for my assistance in the process.

Others find me when their lives have fallen apart with change and I find them in the "Dark Night of the Soul" where they are experiencing post-change trauma and often need serious energy therapy and then a second series helping them to re-create their lives... often from scratch!

Here are some areas of change that might fall into both of the categories that I mentioned:

### Fundamental Change:
- Client wants to change something at the core of who he/she is.
- Giving up an old habit or attachment to a lifestyle or life pattern.
- This relates to personal mission and values...

### Relevatory Change:
- Client allows something in his personality/SELF to come out for the first time.
- Client is finally deciding to shift and be AUTHENTIC... and be in personal balance with him/herself.

### Habitual Change:
- Shifting something that is not working.
- Changing both personal and professional habits, patterns, cycles so that life can be improved.

## STEPS OF CHANGE

Change never happens "over night"! Whether you consciously know it is coming or plan it does not matter... change will occur.

Here are some indicators and steps that you can guide your client to take when they are appropriate:

- Recognition that change is occurring. Being conscious about the situation, gauging emotions about the change, and taking necessary energy therapy steps when needed.

- "Factual dis-engagement from the past"... recognizing that there is a new way and that change IS HAPPENING. Accepting that life is not going to be the same as before. Just ACCEPTING... and using energy therapy if this is a struggle.

- "Emotional dis-engagement from the past"... recognizing that the past is over... and bringing the emotions and feelings of being NOW into the PRESENT. Help the client to untangle the energy and emotions. Help them move beyond the nostalgia or yearning for the past. Help them become skillful in the use of various energy therapy tools, and coach them to use these when they need them!

- Identifying the change and seeing the anticipated results of that change. Client continues to process the emotions so that he/she will be ready for when the results really occur. This is where positive results can be "tapped" into the meridians to help crystallize the results. Identifying the interim steps that must be taken from the point of recognition to the final results of the change.

- Be in the moment of the change to recognize, learn, move forward, understand the opportunities of the change. Help your client to look at different aspects of the change and see it from various perspectives... and remind them to tap when necessary.

- Internalize the lessons of change. Guide your client to see the benefits and guideposts along the way so that the opportunities become clearer to the client. Also support your client to see when the results/goal of the change is almost reached. Help them make the best of the situation... the goal is almost accomplished, and it is time to move on. (This is the last phase of the change... and new change is on its way.)

## Self-Coaching Tools To Help Oneself Through Change

These self-help tools will help your client (or anyone going through change) to feel better, move through the transition more gracefully, and to take the most positive and beneficial steps in the change process.

- Focus on identifying that change is occurring.
- Focus to be able to communicate the results of the change. Talking about what the results of the change will be will support a deeper understanding and acceptance. "Tap" the feelings of the results into your electro-magnetic biofield.
- Focus on which personal strengths will support the process.
- Identify and concentrate on the positive ESSENCE(s)[26] that they will feel when the results of change occur. Running this feeling into the vibration and tapping it in daily will support and accelerate the change process.
- Focus on potential actions that can be taken to move the change forward and help in the transition. Identifying the "baby steps" that can move oneself forward gently and positively. Listen for the "inspired actions" and be conscious of the traditional 80% "busy steps" that need not be taken to gain the desired results.
- Find and USE a support network of friends, family, peers, formal help support groups, etc.
- Focus on what IS WORKING. Savor and celebrate the breakthroughs and milestones... and tiny little shifts that feel good.
- Be alert to plateaus or stalls in forward movement through the change. Be able to notice and then get back into the change process, focusing on the essences of the desired results.
- Create a personal ritual around the change. Let go of the

---

[26] Refer back to **Step 3** for the **Vibrational Essence Exercise**.

old with ceremony, and release what doesn't fit the new situation/life anymore.

- Remember to clear old energy as you let it go using smudging, sound, light, fresh air, and other clearing processes.
- Understand that it is OK TO BE OUT OF CONTROL!! Use energy therapy and personal ways to release tension and ALLOW.
- Guide your client to allow him/herself to FEEL and move through the change... and to use the energy therapy tools whenever the feeling is uncomfortable.
- Daily journaling can help a person going through change to document the shifts, release the emotions, keep sight of the goal, and celebrate the positive aspects of the change.
- Help to identify that change (good or bad) is natural... and the process is controllable and repeatable. Change doesn't have to HURT if the attitude and approach is positively controlled.
- Making the BEST of the situation and understanding the process as it unfolds, allows a person to maintain his/her personal power. This is determined by how a person controls his/her thoughts, attitudes, and resulting emotions.
- "Somehow, some way this is going to be OK!!" This can be a powerful personal mantra... and if there is the tiniest bit of disbelief or doubt, then tapping can clear that resistance.

SELF COACHING is the key to dealing with change... and will make the biggest difference in your clients' lives. Clients want to follow a guide with a system, and they will follow you as you point out to your clients that their coaching experience with you will benefit them in the future with tools that they can use whenever new change comes up.

# Creating More Results While Applying Simplicity

We must always be in INTEGRITY. Clients are attracted to your true ESSENCE or the frequency at which you are vibrating... the energy you are putting out.

You must walk your talk in order to coach people to change. And, the understanding and adoption of the process of change are necessary before the areas of simplifying and creating balance can be implemented. Change leads the process, then one can go forward with creating the foundation to create the life that is most beneficial and successful for the more-evolved individual.

## SIMPLICITY

First a client must "get" the process of change... then he/she may be ready for simplifying. And, when one simplifies life, then processes flow more easily, less thinking is necessary, less stress is present, life is easier.

### Good Questions for your client:
- What would be different if your life were simple??
- What would you get if your life were simple?

Simplicity assists to better develop a person on his/her evolutionary path. Simplicity creates more time, energy, space, income, clients, etc. Think of it as "clearing the space" to allow more in.

*Guide your clients through the following exercise questions as you support them to understand the concept and Simplify their lives:*

- So, how do you feel NOW??? Is your life "easy" to live as it is right now??

- What would it feel like to have a simpler life now??

- What would you REALLY like to simplify about your life now??

- What are ALL the areas that take more time, energy, money and create stress in your life now??

- What does "simplicity" mean to you - feel like, look like??

## Steps to SIMPLICITY:

Coach your client to make a list of all areas that can be simplified in his/her life. You may create a special journal worksheet for the client and support them in tapping to become clearer.

For each area of your client's life that needs to be simplified, have him/her fill out the Goal-planning Exercise.[27]

Ask the client which area he/she wants to begin simplifying first.

When this is simplified, then ask for the client's next priority area.

[This process can keep your clients involved with you well beyond the first contract. You become the "personal life trainer" for your client and continue to take this person on to each next level as it comes up.]

---

[27] Find this in **Appendix 7**.

## Achieving and Managing BALANCE

Balance is a necessary part of every function and aspect of life.

Related to change, balance is discovered through guiding one's way out of contrast, resistance, dis-ease to find an emotional and mental sense of equilibrium. All levels of life and being must be in balance for you and your clients.

So, the questions all relate to HOW you can help your clients move from the place of contrast (in any area of life), using the intention of balance and harmony, into balance and wholeness. The "juggling act" must end so that balance and harmony can be reached and maintained.

Remember that as a coach you must find your own balance first. Only you as an individual (and your client when he or she reaches this ability level) can step off the imbalance merry-go-round to find balance... and sometimes even you may need a coach or energy therapist to help you get back into balance!! Here are some questions to ask yourself and your client:

## STEPS TO BALANCE Exercise:

- Is there a "juggling act" going on that creates stress??
- Is the person too harried to take time for him/herself??
- Are there any signs in the lifestyle that this person is out of balance??
- How does the client talk – what words do they use regularly??
- Is the person able to step off the life routine and relax - or are they STUCK in HIGH??
- Are there themes or patterns that are causing stress in life?? (Regular tardiness, harried energies, disorganizations, victim identity, stressed, exhausted,

broken agreements, forgetfulness, dis-ease in any way, etc.)

Often people are out of balance in one or many parts of their lives. A coach or observer may find this obvious, while the person may not realize it at all.

### *Guide your client through the following questions:*

- Are you feeling stressed or harried in any area of your life now??

- Do you have any re-occurring patterns or themes in your life that are un-beneficial to you??

- What would it feel like to change the area(s) of dis-ease in your life??

- What would it take to create balance in this area(s) now??

## Guidelines and Boundaries to Support Balance in Life

**Guideline =** something one sets up to guide his/her behavior. A guideline helps a person's decision-making process. These may define who he/she is.

### *Ask your client:*

- Where would creating and setting a guideline make your life and decision-making processes easier??
- What guidelines would support you to create new processes that will de-stress your life as it is now?
- Which guidelines will help you to reach your goals faster?

When the guideline is identified, then have your client adopt it and try it out for a week or so. If it works, then it can become a habit. If it is not effective, then it can be shifted and the new guideline can then be tried. Using this gradual process enables a client to adopt something with which he or she resonates instead of creating a rule that has many "should's" attached from others.

When one guideline is established and it works to create the desired changes, then it can be considered successful... until it needs to be adapted because of other changes around it.

**Boundary =** something one sets up to guide another's behavior. Boundaries are set so that a person's life can change while feeling somewhat "protected" from certain behaviors of others. Setting and communicating boundaries is a very freeing and potent process, and is often very new for some people.

### Ask your client:

- Where would setting a boundary on another make your life and environment easier??
- What boundaries would give you the security that you need as you move forward through and beyond change in your life?

It is important in this area to support your client to set and take actions to enforce boundaries in his/her life around any aspect that feels the least bit vulnerable.

### Guide your client through the following questions:

- What or who are the ENERGY DRAINS in your life now - personal life, family, work group, society, community, etc.?? (Could this be because you need to set boundaries here??)

- What boundary would benefit you to set now, based on where you are today??

- How would you benefit by setting this boundary??

- How is the best way to communicate your boundary to the other(s) involved... so that you feel safe as you communicate it??

Again, after setting a boundary, it is important to try it on for a week or so and then "tweak" it if necessary. Creating a "behavior request" with its implications if the boundary is broken, is important and requires the support of a coach.

Change must be understood before moving on with these more intricate steps.

Change must be co-created with your client.

Simplicity, Balance, Agreements, & Boundaries are very personal and, while they benefit from a coach's assistance, they must all be identified and supported by the client... with the foundation of an understanding of the change process.


***So, to pull this Step in the coaching process all together for your client, guide him/her through the following:***

What is one area of your life that you commit to **simplify** NOW??

What is one area of your life where you will focus on **balance** NOW??

- What is one **guideline** that you will set for your own behavior to improve your life NOW??

- What is one **boundary** that you will set and

communicate to improve your quality of life NOW??

When your client has LIVED these concepts then they can share them with others!!

## Practical Applications for YOU:

As in other steps and sections, go through all of the client questions in this area and ask them of yourself. When you truly model the concepts, then you can be a more effective coach to your clients.

# Step 13 – Understanding and Working Beyond Fears

As an energy therapist this section is something you already know about, but by pointing out specifics of fear here you may be able to go even deeper with clients.

Your job is to support your client to "peel the onion" so that in each session he or she can leave feeling lighter and less blocked to moving forward in life.  Since FEAR is the biggest blocker of forward motion, it usually plays a part of all emotional issues that might hold a client back from reaching and enjoying the results of goals.

On the Pre-coaching form that my clients fill out prior to each session I ask about the issue that is up for the client and what he wishes to cover in this next session. Even though I don't specifically ask about "fear" per se, it is usually hiding somewhere in the client's coaching intention for the day.

As you get into each coaching session you may find some resistance or inner struggle, and in examining that in the client you may wish to ask something like:

- What are some of the fears that you have now?
- What about this situation brings up fear?
- What are you afraid of related to this issue?

As a coach, people will come to you because they want to make a change, and they either don't think they can do it, or they haven't been able to yet.

It is important for you to help your client to surface up their fears because this is an area where people need a coach's support. Whenever someone wants to embark upon something new, it is your role to first remind them to initiate their vision, to look at the essences of what they want to feel around that vision. Next you will lead them to identify their blockages – including underlying fears.

***Guide your client to think about the vision. (If this needs to be updated, then ask them to repeat the Multi-Sensory Vision exercise so that it reflects them at the present stage of development.)*[28]**

- When we look at your vision I want you to feel all of your senses.
- Keeping your vision in mind, focus on the feeling of your essences. Do these fit with your vision?
- What will you feel when you hold your vision?

Next, ask your client to look at any doubts, feelings of inner resistance, or blocks that come up while looking over the vision. These "yeah but's" or self-imposed mental arguments set up resistance to success. Get your client to feel these. Ask if the feelings show up in some part of the body as a resistance or other physical sensation.

Next, guide your client to go deeper to find the fears related to the inner doubts. One of the most important things to get from this session is to first recognize, and then be okay with fear... knowing that energy therapy tools can clear the sensations and then allow the client to move forward.

Fear is an opportunity to look more deeply into self. There is no judgment necessary. Just the ability to be okay with feeling afraid can be a major step for some individuals.

Often fear is something that is held back – society teaches us to hide our emotions – especially fear. Nobody likes to admit to having fears. To be able to help a client move through fear you first have to help them let it be okay that they're afraid. Once you can assist your client to be okay with where they

---

[28] See **Appendix 5** for this exercise.

are, then you can help them to take the next step.

It is important to take very small, practical, safe steps when moving through fear. (What we cover here in this section is best used for basic life fears. In the case of PTSD / Post Traumatic Stress Disorder, the protocol alters and should be handled by only very skilled experts in that field.) When your client is thinking about his/her fears and blockages it is necessary to focus first on the fear and then on the small actions that will take your client beyond his/her fear. Some of these actions include using energy therapy tools and setting personal Agreements and Boundaries.

## Moving Through Fear

Guide your client through the following steps:

1- Have your client focus on his/her vision.

2- What blockages or fears or doubts or "yeah but's" arise around this vision?

3- What are the essences that your client wants to FEEL around this vision?

4- Have your client let it be okay that they have a fear. One of the first steps of moving through fear is acknowledging that there is a place of fear.

5- As your client thinks about a particular fear help him or her get a sense of getting into that fear and letting it surface. Help them identify the blockage that keeps them from reaching their vision and feeling their chosen essences.

6- As the fear comes up guide your client to use energy therapy tools to clear any unpleasant feeling associated with the fear or issue bringing it up.

7- Ask your client to dig in and go deeper to identify the basis or root cause for the fear. This is like peeling an onion. When a client hasn't gotten to the root of the fear it can disable their ability to reach goals because there is something that blocks progress.

8- Ask your client to tell you more about the fear:
   a. On a scale of 0-10 how strong is it?
   b. What other emotions are related to the fear?
   c. Where is it felt in the client's body?
   d. When is the first time that your client has ever felt a fear such as that?
   e. What is similar or different about that first situation?
   f. Have there been a series of similar situations that elicit this kind of fear?

9- Ask powerful questions such as above to invoke a deeper insight into the fear and to identify whether this is part of a recurring negative cycle that brings up fear.

Helping your clients to move through fear is about feeling around in the energy to find a place for a little vibrational shift upward. When this is identified the next step is to dissipate the fear by getting it all out and working through it step by step using energy therapy tools. Once you've helped your clients to surface and clear their fear they can then dissipate the energy around it and move forward in their lives!!

One of the most important things for you as a coach is to hold a vision for your clients that they CAN move through fear and that moving through fear is of great value to them.

Think about times you've moved through fears yourself, when you have had something you've been afraid of. If you can come from the intention that you are going to take baby steps to move through fears, then the momentum of the energy of those actions begins to start, giving you the confidence for success as you consciously apply energy therapy tools to clear the emotional charge.

## Advanced Self Coaching Skills

Every human experiences FEAR. It is a major life motivator for many people. It can push even the strongest person out of balance.

Fear of <u>not having</u> or <u>not being</u> something is a motivator that creates actions, habits, phobias, etc. Some of the common fears include:

- being alone (not having companions),
- being left out (not being included),
- Illness (lack of health),
- Dependence (lack of confidence to be independent),
- not knowing enough (ignorance),
- not getting it right,
- not Being enough,
- rejection (not being accepted),
- not having enough money, work, clients, etc.

It is important to keep your clients from being "driven" by fear, and to be more in control without being manipulated by fear.

Advanced Coaching and self-coaching tools that dis-empower FEAR and substitute the essences of wisdom, peace of mind, and happiness include:

1-Identifying what is up for you or your client.
2-Applying coaching tools to assist with the four FEAR areas of:

- Money
- Left-overs
- Truth

- Self-beliefs

## The Four Major Fear Areas:

**1. Money** is a major trigger in our society. This can involve lack of money as well as too much money and the responsibilities/fears associated with having so much. Marital problems and issues within relationships often are based around differing attitudes and fears about money. Often people stay in jobs or work settings that they hate or that are dangerous to their health – just for the money. One's relationship with money is what will release the fear around it.

***Ask your client:***

- What do you FEAR about money??
- Do you have any money issues??
- Describe them:

One good exercise is to have your client write a letter to "money" as though it were a person. In creating a personal relationship with money and understanding that it is just paper and a means of exchange, your client can diffuse its control over her and her fear of it. This is a fun exercise through which to guide your client. She can change her emotional attitude about money by creating a fun working relationship with it and telling it exactly how she feels!!

There are many energy therapy tools that you can also use with your client to clear all aspects of issues with money. Personalize your approach with each client.

**2. Eliminating "Left-overs"** is the next issue. You can imagine an old container left in the back of your refrigerator. You know it has been in there for a very long time. It is taking up space in the refrigerator, may create mold or rot in other things there, might result in an unpleasant situation as you clean it up (or not), and is getting worse the longer it stays in the refrigerator.

This is the same as an old issue, an old possession, old papers/files, un-finished business of any kind that has not been resolved or with which you haven't yet had closure. This is subconsciously taking your energies and producing nothing positive. It is definitely a time for action to let go of this emotional, psychological, or other baggage. You or your client will be glad you did!

### Guide your client through the following steps:

1- Notice that the "left-over" is there taking up space in your psyche or surroundings. Decide to take some definitive action on it at last. It has been draining your energy and it is time for you to do something about this.

- Do you have an emotional, energetic, or physical "left-over" that is taking up space in your life?? What is it??

2- Next is a step where you shift your attitude toward the "left over" so that you can approach it to resolve it and clear the energy (or the rotten item in the refrigerator). Remember, that it will sit there and grow until you resolve to shift something.

- Do you have any resistance to letting go and resolving or releasing your "left-over"?? Describe how you feel about this:
- Tap away any emotions that may be blocking you.

3- Next is the step of taking action to "eliminate a left-over once and for all". This is the action of taking the intention from step 2 and putting action behind it.

- What are you going to do in order to release and have closure with your "left-over"??

**3. Inviting TRUTH into your life** is the next step. This helps your client to meet his or her "authentic self". When one is not "authentic", then they lose their own personal power and don't feel good about themselves.

It is important to coach your client to identify WHO they are, and what they really WANT to do and BE... not only on a big scale, but in simple little daily actions, habits, dress codes, etc.

### Guide your client to answer the following:

- List some of your personal "truths" that you have not been honoring up to now, and that you can begin to focus on putting back into your life so that you will be more authentically "YOU".
- What aspect of yourself has been missing and now you wish to call it back?
- Do you feel any resistance around living in your full TRUTH? If so, then clear it with energy therapy!

**4. Letting go of Inhibiting Self-Beliefs** is the final area of focus here. In letting go of the blockages that often exist in personal self-beliefs you can move toward reaching your full potential and identifying your own GREATNESS.

Your core coaching skills of listening, supporting, empowering, helping your client find his/her greatness will identify limitations in self-beliefs. With this realization you can guide your client through the process of changing these inner beliefs. This is where skilled basic coaching will support your client to shift to a much different level to create a life only dreamed of before.

It is a process of taking a person from focusing on "what they are NOT" to taking them to focusing on "what they ARE". Helping your client to shift his /her perception, create new positive thought processes, speech patterns, verbage used, attitudes about him or herself will help to create the desired life.

## It's all about Vibration!

As you start coaching your clients to take those small action steps and move up the scale vibrationally, they begin to feel a greater sense of confidence in their ability to move through fear. They start getting bolder about the fears that they're willing to move through. It is best to start tackling smaller level fears so that little by little the clients start to feel lighter, and can feel the shifts with each step they take. As larger fears rise to the surface of their unconscious mind they will already have a pattern of feeling vibrationally better, so part of them will look forward to having that uplifting feeling after clearing the next fear that is in the way.

## Practical Applications for YOU:

Walk yourself through the steps above to identify a fear in your life at this time. Peel the onion around this fear issue so that you can begin to dissipate the negative feelings and blockage created by the fear. Apply your own favorite energy therapy tools and start to feel the vibrational lightening. Go through the questions listed in this section to assist you in looking at all the layers of your issue.

*Do you have any fears about coaching your clients around this issue of fear??*

# Step 14 – Creating Your Inspired Life!

It is my personal philosophy that life is all about the search for personal fulfillment. I often feel in awe of my own profession as Energy Therapist/ Coach, since our job is to guide and support this essence of life itself in our clients and others.

This section is merely a reminder of how profound our work is and how we can benefit as we guide others forward on their own paths.

So many of the exercises in this Guidebook provide tools to attain that Inspired Life full of Peace, Happiness, Passion, Love. Who needs more than that?

## Seeking Fulfillment

Often clients come to us seeking a sense of Fulfillment in some aspect of their life. This section will help you to take your clients well beyond "surviving" in their lives to a high degree of "thriving" in all areas of life... and then you will be able to support them to do this on their own.

Most clients want something new – they want something to change – they want to feel differently. They wish to drop the barriers of their life in order to discover the joy factor and shift their feelings to a higher vibration of contentment, fulfillment, and passion, which will positively affect ALL areas of their lives.

If a survey were taken, there would probably be strong quantitative evidence that those who succeed most in their lives do so because they have a high degree of contentment in their lives.

As your clients go deeper into themselves, clearing resistance as they go, they can plant seeds of positive energy to support living PEACE, HAPPINESS, PASSION, and the Inspired Life. And, you can support your clients into QUIET, TRANQUILITY, and inner PEACE as they re-discover their passion and ground a strong sense of contentment and fulfillment.

## Happiness

The JOY factor that you can support in your client makes a difference in ALL areas of his or her life. And, no matter how advanced you or your client may be, there is always a higher level to aspire to reach. So, the process is to set and reach goals, clearing along the way, and then celebrate the move to the next level before moving onward. By capturing and maintaining these high vibrational feelings your client begins to recognize and apply one of the most potent ways to continue evolving.

When a client feels happy he/she will set guidelines and boundaries in his/ her life to keep that feeling. It is not only a motivator but it also supports a person to play in a bigger league – to move to a more advanced level. And, remember – as a coach, you MUST be in a higher place yourself before you can guide your client there. So, these are great skills to support in your own self-coaching and in that of your clients.

## Passion

When one wants more meaning in life, what he/ she is seeking is Passion. People seek more passion in experiences, in connections with others, in the level of love achieved in relationships, and in every other area of life. When they finally discover that passion they encounter emotions that are both invigorating and that feel GREAT!!

### Ask your client:

- Where to you want to feel more PASSION in your life??
- What needs to be changed in order for you to feel more passion there?
- What is holding you back now from going there?

The awareness of where passion needs to be more balanced is the best place to start. Then there are various questions that you can ask your client in order to build passion, fuel it, grow it in all aspects of life.

## An Inspired Life

An Inspired Life is full of Spirit, Enchantment, and Magic! People who have shifted their vibration to a high frequency and who are in touch with their JOY, HAPPINESS, PEACE, LOVE, ABUNDANCE, etc. will evidence MAGIC, special occurrences, "GOOD LUCK", and evidences that they are "in the flow". This is to what we all aspire!

### Ask your client:

- Is your life Inspired?

- What are the evidences that you are sending out the "right" energy for creating an Inspired Life for yourself??

- What are the Inspired aspects or experiences that you have witnessed recently in your life?? List them below:

# Step 15 – Overview of Coaching / Energy Therapy Process

During the last or penultimate coaching/ energy session scheduled with a client it is important that you go back through your notes and focus on your client's accomplishments during the time you have worked together. Showing the client how far he or she has come since the original session, measuring the change from the original "critical gap", and gauging the emotional tone and vibration now versus when he/she first came to you with needs will empower your client to believe in herself or himself. It will also lead to referrals and possibly to future sessions with the client.

The protocol outlined in this section is one that fits right into the coaching curriculum, as coaches thrive on the longevity of their relationship with a client. Some coaches work with the same clients for many years – possibly throughout a client's career, for example.

On the other hand, an energy therapist generally works with a client who needs assistance immediately, and when the goals are met there may or may not be another layer that requires attention with coaching support.

Then, considering the practicalities of running a Coaching/ Energy Therapy practice, it is always nice to have a good client who you already know decide to continue working with you for a long-term commitment to change.

In any of these cases this section provides an empowering wrap-up for a coaching/ energy therapy series with a client, and will support that client to move forward from where you end this series... with or without your further assistance. In doing this you create a win-win situation where both you and the client are winners at the end.

## Discussion Points and Workshop Samples:

The intention for this last session is to talk with your client and share with them that this is the end of their present series, and that you would like to use this session to discuss what occurred during your time together and focus on what the client has accomplished.

You talk to your client about what he has accomplished, and share what you've seen him accomplish. We always hold a picture for our clients outside of the client – that is one of the roles of being a coach.

During this session you also ask the client to share what HE feels he accomplished, and you share your perspective of that too because you hold a different, bigger vision.

An additional thing that you do in this session with the client is to have him look over the Goal Planning Exercise(s) that he has completed during the coaching series. You may want to request prior to the session for your client to bring the exercises to this session for review.

During the session you talk about what has been fulfilled – what goals have been accomplished. You may also point out how the client's critical gap on each goal narrowed with each step or stage of your work together.

Finally, you can end the session with the client talking about his vision, about what else he may desire, what else he might want to accomplish in the future. And then, just co-create and go from there for the rest of the session.

***Here is a sample script for a final session with your client:***

"It is amazing to me that we have gone through our journey together already. It has gone quickly, been enjoyable, and you have progressed so much. My intention for our session today is to spend some time looking at what you have accomplished. I'd like you to get out a piece of paper and a pen and think back over the last eight months. Talk to me as you're writing about what you have accomplished. And client, I don't want you to just think about the big things like, I lost 22 pounds, I got a promotion, or I started my own business. I want you to think about the little things too: the fact that you repaired the relationship with your friend Mary with whom you weren't speaking; the fact that you finally treated yourself to a hair-do that you enjoy; the fact that you were able to have that conversation with your boss that you've never felt comfortable doing before. I want you to think back through everything you have accomplished during our coaching series together."

Just sit and listen as your client writes and speaks. Prod them to make a conscious effort to look at all areas of their life. Most clients will look at what they have experienced in only some areas.

Your job as a coach is to spend time letting them acknowledge themselves and then help them fill in the gaps by telling them what else you see, sharing your observations, sharing your truths, and helping by asking questions to expand them to see other areas. What about this? What about that? What about the work you do in the community? What about how you helped in the soup kitchen on Thanksgiving?

Often you will have clients go through lists of things they accomplished and they are all excited. They will go on and on, and then they will find the one thing that will drag them into the "what's not right" and "what's not working" energy. This is NOT the place nor time to focus on what they DID NOT ACCOMPLISH.

As a coach you must notice if your client slips at all into the negative doubting energy so that you can stop the client and bring him/her back. Ask them questions like:

- What were you proud of?
- When did you feel proud?
- What happened with your relationships that you feel good about?
- What about your eating habits?
- What about your attitude?
- What about your self care?
- What did you learn this year; what did you learn in these months together?
- What kind of skills did you pick up?
- What did you let go of?
- What did you give up?

You keep him in this positive energy of accomplishment for a while. To do this you keep peeling the onion and keep asking:

- What else?
- What about your wealth?
- What about your health?
- What about your relationship to something greater outside of yourself?
- What about your spirituality?

You have him talk about his accomplishments and you ask some probing questions about how he FEELs about these.

You look from outside of that person, and,... you share with him what you see.

Next you ask the client to <u>acknowledge him or herself</u>. First we talked about the accomplishments, now the next coaching skill is self-acknowledgement. You get your client to pat him or herself on the back.

***Say to your client:***

- Do you understand how much you accomplished in this time we have been working together? Do you really get it?
- I want you to acknowledge yourself.
- I want you to celebrate.
- I want you to take a minute and feel good about YOU.

It is your goal to help your client understand and FEEL – that he/ she has come a long way in a short time.

Remember that these are potent self-coaching skills that your clients can use all the time. They can look at their lives and see what they've accomplished. They can see what their actions are and what their essences are.

Next in this session you ask your client about the <u>things she has learned</u>. Ask her:

- During our coaching time together what new skills did you learn?
- What new abilities did you incorporate into practice?
- What coaching skills did you learn?
- What self-coaching skills did you activate within yourself?
- What is a different skill, ability, positive habit that you have now that you didn't have before?

Next have your client <u>take out her goal planning exercises</u>. Get your copy out and say: "Let us take a look at where you were."

If she has more than one goal exercise, work with her in the order of their priority. Review the goals, the processes used to achieve them, and the final results. Then,…

### Ask this powerful question:

"What are three other issues or areas of your life, your health, your wellness, your communication, your finances, your spirituality, (any other aspect of your life) that would make the biggest shift in your life if you accomplished a change there??"

Coach her around what she comes up with, and ask for details:
- How would x impact your life?
- How would you feel if you did x??

What you are doing here is helping your client to create a new vision. You are going back to what you did in the beginning of this program and helping her to create a Technicolor vision, and to clearly SEE it and FEEL it.

That's what you want to do: take her into the Technicolor Vision, where she uses all of her senses to taste it, touch it, feel it, smell it, hear it, fully experience it, and describe every detail of it to you. All you are doing is asking the questions, and that is out of curiosity and care for your client.

Be with your client and let her vision; feel it, love it. See it with her and support her excitement. After she's given you at least three areas where future improvement would impact her life, keep listening and prodding to go deeper into the feelings of the vision or goal.

### After this you can complete the session by saying:

"Based on what you just said, and based on those other areas, those other goals, on what else you want in your life, can you narrow it down with me and tell me the one or two burning goals that if we chose to work together over the next months, would be the goals you chose to work on?"

Obviously you are not saying to the client that he/she has to continue working with you. By now your client has energy therapy tools to use on her own and feels empowered to do several levels of self-coaching. You are providing a further service here in helping to get her on track to move into the future so that she doesn't become stagnant.

And, what you are also saying is for your client to look at the possibility that if she chooses at the end of the call to commit to more coaching, you may help her with the "burning goals" she would choose to work on. Here you are helping her to get clarity.

**You can guide your client toward clarity with comments such as:**

- "So, the burning goals you would work on next would be WHAT?"
- How will the results feel?
- How will your life essences fit into these future goals?
- Etc.

Listen to what those burning goals are and see how you might be able to support your client in the future as a coach/ energy therapist. Often at this point the client has evolved to such an extent that a whole new life is opening up to him or her. New changes must be orchestrated, relationships nurtured, projects undertaken that would never have been on the agenda when you first started working together.

Show your client how the two of you can work on these new specific items/goals together. If he/ she wants to continue with your help and co-creatively work toward achieving these burning goals over the next months, tell them how you will work with him/ her and support him/ her on the goals.

**The essence of the very end of this call is:**

"Would you like to work on these goals together for another coaching series? "

If the client says yes, great, keep them on the schedule.

If the client says they want to think about it, invite them to think about it, and request that they think out loud with you, to tell you what questions and concerns they have right then.

If they say no or they want to take a break for a while, be agreeable. Tell them that you know they can find you and that you would love to assist them to accomplish these goals. And, make the request that if they know anybody like themselves that might replace them while they're taking a coaching break, you would love to have a client just like them. Ask if a referral of somebody you can serve comes to mind. Give this referral a complimentary consult for free as a gift from you.

Following this protocol you might consider this last session of a program to be the Birth of a New Beginning.

## SUMMARY

Here are the steps you can lead your client through during this last session in the coaching series. Ask your client:

- What have you accomplished?
- How are you going to celebrate what you've accomplished?
- What have you learned from our coaching?
- Make a review of the goal planning exercises
- Ask the question; "What are three areas in your life that make the biggest impact on you?"
- Help them do a Technicolor Vision of what it would be like if they achieved the goals in those areas.

- Then have them narrow it down to one or two burning goals to accomplish over the next several months.
- If it is appropriate, suggest that you work on those goals together.
- Give them ideas on how you will support them to reach their goals.
- Invite them to continue as your client and/or refer someone else to you!!

## Practical Applications for YOU:

Congratulate yourself on a job well done. Whether or not your client signs up to continue working with you, if you have followed the program described in this manual, then you have helped another human being to evolve to a new level. That is truly an accomplishment for which you should feel proud and fulfilled!!

## Appendix 1
## Pre-Coaching Intake Form

*For:_____ Birth date:_____*

*First Session Date: _____ Payment Method:_____*

*Phone:_____ _E-mail:_____*

*Familiar with EFT? Yes ____No*
*Utilize it regularly? Yes ____No_____*

In your own words, what is your main priority issue or condition for scheduling a session or series?  How long have you been suffering from this?

If any, what resistance, emotional charge, or challenge do you feel around the above? (ie: Fear? Stress? Frustration? I doubt I can do it? Embarrassed to talk about it?  Etc.) -Describe:

Rate the emotional charge you feel about your priority issue : _____

[0=none/ neutral…. 5= medium charge…. 10=high/ totally stressed]

List all of the specific Emotional Issues or Physical Symptoms you are experiencing right now.

 Now rate each issue on the above list by emotional charge/ physical discomfort using the 0-10 scale listed above.

Provide a list of all medications, supplements, or homeopathic remedies you are presently taking... and add what condition each is treating.

**Describe your present diet:** (non-gluten, paleo, OG/ non-GMO, vegetarian, vegan, traditional southern, etc.)

**Briefly describe your own Spiritual or Religious belief system**: (I regularly attend a Catholic/Protestant/Jewish/other service, I meditate, I feel connected with Spirit/God/Angels/The Universe, I have my own Spiritual feelings, I pray to ___, I am a member of a Spiritual community, etc.) [This is helpful to me as I customize your program for you.]

**List here anything you know about the following from the time of your conception through age 10:** (Parent's attitudes about pregnancy with you, mother's pregnancy experience, traumas during pregnancy, early living environment & setting, socio-economic issues, temperaments of parents, over-all tone of your early life, repeated actions, comments, complaints, declarations by others around you, etc.)

It will be helpful in our work if you list all accidents, physical issues/illnesses, negative emotional life-impacting episodes, surgeries, etc. that have impacted your mind, body, spirit. (You don't need to go into great detail... just list your age and then: "car accident", "divorce", "disappointment", "miscarriage", "job lay-off or lost contract", etc.)

Threats or Challenges that you are facing now in your life -

(What's holding you back?):

Opportunities, insights, and breakthroughs available to you now – (What/Who is supporting you?):

What is your main intention for the <u>results</u> of our first session together?

[This is a perfect place for you to insert an additional form related to your practice or modalities that you use - such as I have done here.]

To provide more information about your body's energetics, please go to *http://wellnesscheckonline.com* . <u>You must use a computer rather than ipad or phone for this.</u>  Then...

**Fill in** the questions listing frequency of feelings & symptoms. (Remember that your body & mind are intricately connected, so the data will guide me whether your issue is physical or not.)

**Submit** and you will receive the results automatically.

<u>**Print out**</u> the two results pages and have available during your first session.

**Use the "Send Results to Practitioner" option** and forward to *info@arielagroup.com* prior to our first session. **Send** the answers on this form to me prior to your session to save time in your session.

Please return this info to:  *Dr. Anne Merkel – info@arielagroup.com* . .. and remember to forward the results of the on-line *Wellness Check* to this e-mail too!

Please mark your areas of pain on the attached diagram...
scan and send, or describe in your first session. Thanks!

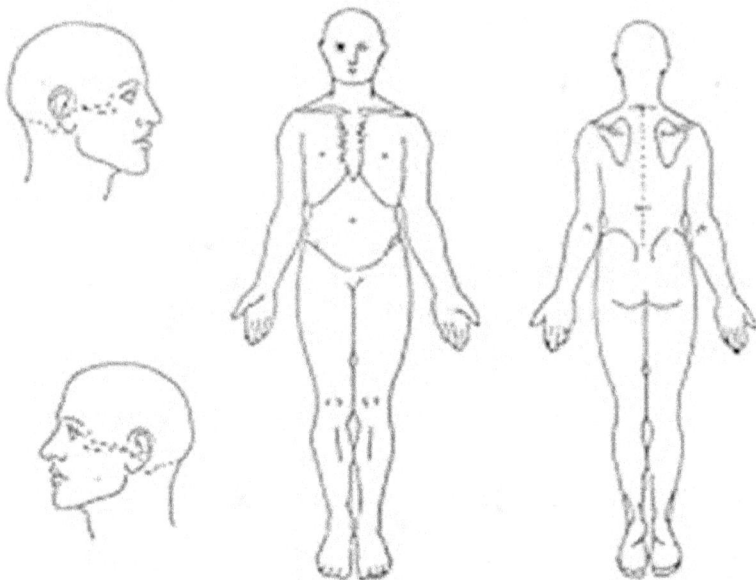

Do you have any questions for me about the energy therapy
sessions I offer, or your first session? *Ask here or contact me
by phone: XXX-XXX-XXXX.*

Thanks!

## Ariela Group Coaching Contract & Policy Statement

It has been our privilege to offer coaching and energy therapy programs for Conscious Transformation since the 1980's. In order to best serve our wide, global audience, we are happy to share here our *Contract & Policy Statement*.

## Registration Agreement:

Your registration for a *Conscious Transformation Coaching Program* is not only a commitment to yourself, but is also seen as your commitment to a contractual agreement with The Ariela Group of Wholistic Services, to work together. If you should prefer to have a separate signed agreement between our two parties, feel free to request one. Otherwise we consider your commitment to register and pay for a program as your official acceptance of the program and its terms.

The Energy Therapy Coaching work that you may contract to receive is begun as soon as you register. You may start to feel shifts before our first session. This is normal because when you register you make an energetic commitment to yourself and to your well-being. And, on our side, as soon as you register we start setting the energy in motion to access your case and focus on your highest priorities.

**Our commitment to you** is to be here for you, to focus on your highest priorities, and to be the purest channel for the modalities that we share so that you can benefit to the utmost.

**Our expectation of you** is that you follow through with the between-sessions energy support for yourself, that you provide both pre- and post-coaching forms before and after each session, that you provide us with the results of an on-line wellness evaluation found at: http://www.wellnesscheckonline.com, and that you understand that you have the power to clear all causes of your discomfort or dis-ease, and that we must be open with each other in order to best support your healing. The more of your history that you share, the deeper the clearing we can accomplish together!

All of your information will be held totally in confidence, and in cases of painful memories or past trauma, we need not know the details or past "story" in order to help you let go of the emotional charge associated with the experience. You do not need to suffer or relive anything painful in order for our work together to be very beneficial and life-changing. And, you need not fear that we would ever "leave you hanging out on a limb" if deep emotions do come up. You will feel comfortable working in the safe environment that we co-create, so you can open up in confidence and feel protected.

Our coaching packages are not priced on an hourly basis, but are labeled with a value for a package of energetic support which may be delivered via phone consultations, recordings thereof, e-mail support, wellness check analyses, e-book support, and face-to-face consultations. There is much behind-the-scenes time and energy support that is involved in the work that we do. This is not quantifiable in the measure of contact hours, but represents an all-encompassing program of treatment for your highest good. Occasionally we decide to change our prices and this is never based on any hourly figure, but is more a wholistic approach to the energetics of our business entity.

Dr. Anne Merkel is a trained and certified Life and Business Coach, NET Practitioner, EFT Practitioner and Trainer, TFH Practitioner of Applied Kinesiology, Reiki Master, and experienced Energy Therapist with satisfied clients world-wide. She has been trained in both science-based as well as more esoteric spiritual energy techniques, and tends to customize her treatment for each unique client experience. She will share with you the wealth of over twenty-five years of both extensive study and hands-on client work. Dr. Merkel has published articles and reports based on the many cases she's treated. Anne is not a physician nor is she a psychologist, although she utilizes Energy Psychology modalities and has been trained in psychology. She earned her MS and Ph.D. degrees from Indiana University and regularly attends advanced seminars and workshops in her chosen modalities.

## Our Policies:

When you made the decision to sign up for a coaching program you may have been offered a full or several payment option for your series, and we are happy to have offered this to you. We cannot switch you from one payment plan to another after you have already registered.

If you signed up for a multi-payment plan your subscription payments are automatically deducted from your payment source on the anniversary date at the specified interval of your subscription. This process is easy on all of us and nobody has access to your accounts except the secure system.

In order to change your contract in any way you must contact us at: *info@arielagroup.com*, in writing and schedule a time when we can meet by phone to discuss your needs or concerns. If we do not hear from you and a payment has been billed automatically, a refund will not be available to you for the new subscription period, however we will be glad to offer products or services to complete the paid subscription. Our thousands of clients have been happy with our services and the results they have felt after experiencing the full process for which they have contracted.

In the rare case when a contract needs to be terminated, our policy is that we will reimburse up to 50% of the amount still left and not yet served on the contract full subscription or package price. For example, if a contract cancellation request is made half-way through a $4000 package, then up to $1000 will be refunded with no questions asked.

It is our desire to support and satisfy our customers, and we realize that every case is totally unique. We appreciate clear communication so that we may together co-create an agreement that will best meet the desires of all parties involved.
We hope that our policies are clear to you and that you enjoy your association with The Ariela Group of Wholistic Services and all of our products and services. If you have any questions about our **Coaching Contract and Policy Statement**, please feel free to **_contact us_**.

## *Appendix 3*
## EFT Tapping Points Video

This video provides the traditional EFT/ Emotional Freedom Technique tapping points as well as a few additional points that I use in my practice and highly endorse to you. After pointing out the tapping locations you will also learn the emotions that generally relate to each tapping point. Enjoy !

Go to:  http://www.myeftcoach.com/alternative-medicine/ for the video.

For a more extensive Introduction to EFT you may go to: http://arielagroup.com/products/free_products.php

## *Appendix 4*
## Pre-Coaching Notes for Energy Therapy Session:

*For:_____Date:_____Next*
*Session #:_____*

*I used EFT since my last session: __Yes __No*

- **How I have felt since our last session:**

- **Change in feelings, attitude, or emotional tone this week:**
    - ○ **Physical:**
    - ○ **Mental:**
    - ○ **Emotional:**
    - ○ **Spiritual:**

- **What I have accomplished since our last session:**

- **What I didn't get done this week, but intended to:**

- **Am I feeling resistance, emotional charge, or challenge around the above? ___Yes ___No**

- **Charge:____ [0=Neutral….5=Medium….10=Upset/Stuck!]**

- **Description of my Feelings about the above:**

- **The challenges and problems I am facing now & wish to resolve:**

- **Opportunities, insights, and breakthroughs available to me now:**

## Post-Coaching Notes for Energy Therapy Session:

*For:*_____*Date:*_____*Sessio
n #:*_____

- **Subtle changes I have noticed since our session:**

    1. **Physical:**

    2. **Mental:**

    3. **Emotional:**

    4. **Spiritual:**

    5. **Other/ Over-all:**

- **High points/ break-throughs of our session:**

- **Questions or feedback about my session, techniques used, feelings, etc.:**

- **Shifts in levels of stress, depression, pain, discomfort, emotional charge, etc.:**

- **What I notice that feels different in my life now:**

- **Goals that I choose to accomplish before the next session:**

- **Opportunities that are now presented with the above goal(s):**

- **Challenges or emotional blocks that I now face with these goal(s):**

- My feelings & thoughts about what I am co-creating in my life:

- Other session notes or ideas that I'd like to remember:

- New tapping issues or feelings around which I will tap now or in a future session:

- Other comments:

## *Appendix 5*
## Multi-Sensory Vision Exercise

A Multi-sensory Vision is a potent tool for intending first, and then attracting what you desire into reality. It is simple and self-driven. It can be projected for a day, 30 days, 6-8 months, a year, 5 years, etc. For the purposes of our coaching together we can focus on 30-day visions, 60-day visions, 90-day visions, 6-month visions, 8-month visions.

To begin you can focus on your whole life in general. Often we push out one year into the future to focus on what one's life will be like in all areas exactly one year from now. This may be a good place to start in this exercise.

Next you will look at all the parts of your life puzzle and create separate Multi-sensory visions for each segment, each goal. It is best to look at different time segments for this process, based on each goal. Some goals are achievable in 30 days. Some goals have various sub-categories that will take less time to manifest, while the entire goal might take a year or longer to achieve. Be realistic as you perform this exercise. And, keep in mind the goals around which you feel emotional resistance that will need to be cleared before moving forward.

As a coach you probably already use this technique for yourself. For your client it is best if you first lead your client through a session where you create the space for them to visualize and build on the vision that they most desire. It need not take long to guide your client through this process.[29] You might want to allow up to 10 minutes for your direction and then another 10-15 minutes to discuss and build on the vision with your client.

_____

[29] For an audio guide to this process go to:
http://ariela.audioacrobat.com/download/MultiSensoryVision_02011 5.mp3

The following points will guide you as you comfortably lead your client in this process. You will do this early in your coaching series and then instruct your client to do it regularly as goals are shifted, added, amped-up.

o   Guide your client to a centered place. Have them stop writing, relax, breath, close their eyes.
o   Direct your client to imagine their life, their business, bank account, personal relationship, education level, job parameters, health, weight, (whatever their focus area might be)... as it will be X months into the future. (This is how life will be after one series of coaching with you.)
o   Remind them of the areas of life that they should include (and this can be all areas or just specific ones, based on your client. – If the client has approached you for specific coaching around one area, then that will be what the vision is about. If the client is looking for an over-all change of life, then all areas are to be impacted through the coaching and this will be reflected in the vision they create.)
o   Have them imagine that they ARE LIVING this vision of X months (or less) into the future.
o   Remind your client to EXPERIENCE the vision and to FEEL all of the senses around each area of the vision. Walk them through each sense and ask:
o   How does it FEEL?
o   What does it look like?
o   What do you smell?
o   What do you hear?
o   Touch the surfaces around you and describe how they feel.
o   What do you feel in your relationships with x, y, z?
o   Etc.
o   Ask them what they will FEEL when their goal(s) have been achieved. What are the "ESSENCES" that they want to feel as they create this life?
o   Remind them that this is a "Multi-sensory vision", so it needs to be REAL, full of flavor and color and feeling sensation, and must be related to their innermost desires

of how they want to FEEL in their desired life.

- Give your client a bit of time to go deeper into the silence and imagine all of the sensory details of their vision.
- Now gently bring your client back into present, reminding them to breathe, and open their eyes.
- Provide a few minutes for them to write down some notes about their vision so that they do not forget.
- Now ask them to describe their vision to you and to go into as much detail as they can. If you generally record or type the coaching session, then you can keep the information to share later with your client... otherwise you can sketch some notes of key points so that you can later review these with your client.
- Guide your client to go deeper within the vision so that it becomes even more detailed and sensory-based as you discuss it.
- Ask prodding questions related to the details and how the client will FEEL around each aspect of the vision.
- Ask your client how he/she feels as they focus and feel the vision. (They should report that they feel light, free, excited, positive, higher vibration than before... and this is what you can remind them to re-visit whenever they feel down or lower in vibration.)
- Make sure that your client records their feelings of lightness, joy, etc. so that they might create a physical "trigger" to return to that feeling or simply learn to manage their thoughts so that they can remind themselves of how good they feel as they focus on this vision that you are going to coach them to achieve.
- Ask your client to take time after the coaching session to record their vision and to go more deeply into each area of the vision.
- Guide your client to divide each area of focus into a separate vision, and to create 30-day goals within each vision. It will be these "bite sized pieces" that will be the focus of future coaching sessions and in-between self-coaching sessions.
- Direct your client to finish their vision(s) right after this

coaching session and to read them regularly to place the energetics and feelings into their mind and heart so they can amp up the magnetic charge to attract what they most desire.

o Also remind your clients now and in future coaching sessions to revise the goals and the vision as time goes by, and to make a separate listing of all of the successes as short-term goals are achieved. Help your client to celebrate these achievements and remind them to list them also in the pre-coaching worksheet that you co-create for each session.

o Finally, guide your client to create a vision around anything and everything that they desire as their life continues to evolve. They can guide themselves in the process after you have introduced them to it and discussed it. It will be an easy tool and one that will provide great happiness and success for your client!!

Even though the process seems long, it is not. You have all of the details here that you need to direct the creation of a wonderful and life-changing Multi-sensory Vision in your client.

You may want to create your own script based on the points above and on the recording, and you can share that with your client and direct him/her to record his/her own voice if that will be helpful.

This tool is flexible – and POTENT!! Enjoy using it and sharing it with your clients!!

## *Appendix 6*
## Personal Autobiography Exercise

When you want to go to a deeper level with your client this is a good exercise to help your client bring his/her life into awareness. This is used regularly by career coaches as they direct their clients to re-create their lives. You will be able to coach your clients to shift in major ways... and... first they need to remember and review from where they have come... and dig up any issues that could potentially hold them back from moving forward.

An easy way to direct your client to create their autobiography is to suggest they go decade by decade and record the major events. For a career focus each decade would include the jobs, positions, tasks, career-related accomplishments that occurred for the client within that time period. For a health-related client the focus can be on health or weight issues and accomplishments, challenges, or activities during each decade. For an entrepreneur each decade can relate to entrepreneurial ventures, stages of business development, etc. For each client the autobiography tone will be different.

*Sometimes sharing a graphic "time line" is a good reminder to your client so they can trigger the old memories and just fill in the categories. See the following example and add to it:  (... and yes, some of our older clients use the upper numbers on the scale too!!)*

**0--10--20--30--40--50--60--70--80--90--100**

- o Infant and early childhood/ primary school
- o Childhood and teens/ primary, middle, high school, college/ first jobs, romances
- o Young adulthood/ college, grad school/ jobs/

relationships/ kids & family
- o Retirement/ Etc.

*Just direct your client to go back and record the important aspects of each decade of their life.*
- o Have them focus on the positive experiences and how they felt.
- o Have them focus on the challenges and what was learned from each one.
- o Discuss this exercise briefly and ask what memories were stirred up and made the most impact for your client. What did they remember that surprised them?
- o Ask your client if there were any patterns in their life that they could see more clearly now after doing the exercise.
- o Ask your client what they learned from the exercise.

*Use this information in future coaching sessions... the more you know, the more you can support your client!!*

*Have fun with this easy process!!*

## *Appendix 7*
## Personal Goal Planning Exercise

This exercise is designed to provide a step-by-step protocol to plan how to achieve important goals.  It is easy to use and, when complete, should provide a road map to take you where you desire. You will receive help with this from your EFT Coach.  At the end you will know what you want to achieve, how long it should take, what you need to get there, and how to measure your progress.

To use this tool, simply answer the questions on the next few pages.  The questions are meant to cause you to think, so you may not have the answer immediately upon reading the question.  The more thoughtful you are in answering the questions, the more complete your plan will be.

Use the protocol for only one goal at a time.  If you have several goals, make copies and go through this process for each goal.  You can then prioritize which goal should be worked on first.

Welcome to planning and achieving your goals faster and easier than before!

# I: Identifying the Goal and It's Importance

*The goal I choose to achieve is:*

*The reason I choose to achieve this goal is:*

**When I reap the rewards of achieving this goal I will feel: (go into detail using each sense as you FEEL the results that you will be experiencing soon.)**

*My life will change in the following manner when I achieve my goal:*

*I will be happier when I achieve this goal because:*

*The answers to the above questions have made me realize that I am truly willing to commit the time, energy, emotions, and resources necessary to achieve my goal:*
_____Yes    _____No

## II:  Clearing Barriers to My Goal

It is imperative that before going further I evaluate whether I am totally congruent with achieving my goal, or not.

*1- As I scan the results that I am attracting as I achieve this goal, do I feel any inner resistance or doubt that I'll be able to achieve it?  And, if so, describe the feelings of resistance and potential causes.*

**2- Now that I have identified some blocks to achieving my desired results, I choose to clear the issues causing the inner resistance. I will list below:**

     **a-the blocks that I feel,**

     **b-potential causes of this blockage,**

     **c-what energy therapy tools I will use to clear this,**

     **d-sample EFT set-up statements that I can use.**

## III. Clarifying the Desire Around the Goal

In cases where the desire or goal is to attract the "right" relationship, new home, job offer, best clients for a practice, new car, etc., the following grid is quite helpful in ensuring that the most beneficial decision is made, and this can be used to clearly state in writing the **MUST HAVE 100% REQUIREMENTS** as well as the **EXTRA DESIRES** that will simply make the final candidate(s) even more enticing.

*Take a piece of paper and draw a line down the middle. On the left of the line is the MUST HAVE 100% category and on the right is the EXTRA CREDIT list.   As candidates, or choices start to turn up within the goal setting process, this is a handy tool that can keep you on target and support clarity in decision-making. [This step may not be necessary for every goal or every client.]*

| MUST HAVE 100% | ADDITIONAL DESIRES |
| --- | --- |
| | |

## IV: Identifying Action Steps Toward My Goal

With the commitment to this goal I choose now to determine what I must do in order to achieve my goal. There are several steps I must take to make my goal a reality.

*After clearing my inner blocks now I can identify some action steps to take so that I can move closer to achieving the results of my goal. This list includes 5-10 proposed action steps toward my goal.*

## V:  All In Divine Timing

Now that I am clear to move forward and I have identified the action steps I will take, I choose to attract inspiration concerning when each step should be taken and how to take it. I expect that all will happen in good timing, and in order to set the energies in motion, I choose to list my action steps below in chronological order with the dates by which I choose to have completed each step:

*Action Step:*                                    *Projected*
*Completion Date:*

## VI:  Calling In the Resources When Needed

In order to achieve the action steps toward my goal, I choose to attract a variety of resources.  I realize I will need to commit time, energy, and emotion to the goal.  There may also be other required resources such as money, technical help, or support from those around me.  In this section, I choose to identify exactly what I need, where each resource will come from, and how I might best attract it.  This will give me a clear blueprint to help me achieve my goal.

*Resource No.1:  <u>Time</u>*

*In order to achieve my goal, I need _____ hours per day/week/month (circle one).  I currently have that time available.  _____Yes _____No.  If I do not have that time currently available, I will create it by:*

*Resource No. 2:  <u>Energy</u>*

*To best achieve my goal, I need physical, mental, emotional energy to work on the goal.  I currently have that energy available.  _____Yes _____No.  If I do not have enough energy currently available, I will create it by:*

*Resource No. 3:  <u>Motivating Drive</u>*

*Special energy is needed to motivate me to work on the action steps and ultimately to achieve my goal. I am currently free of inner blocks in this area. _____Yes _____No. If not, then I will clear the following now using the designated energy therapy tools or EFT set-up statements:*

*I currently have the emotional drive and energetic motivation available. _____Yes _____No. If I do not have what I need in this area, I will create it by:*

*Resource No. 4:* *Financial Support*

*To achieve my goal, I need money in the amount of $_____ as working capital and $_____ in savings so that I can work on my goal free of monetary fear. I currently have that money available. _____Yes _____No. If I do not have that money available, I need to attract $_____ more. Below, I have listed how I will fund my goal, where I will find the money, and what steps I must take to put the money at my disposal:*

*[Feel free to add additional Resources that you may need based on the following template.]*

*Resource No\_\_: _____*

*In order to achieve my goal, I need _____. I currently have this resource available. _____Yes _____No. If I do not have it available, I can get it or create it. Below, I have listed how I choose to create the resource, where I will find the resource, and what steps I have to take to put the resource at my disposal:*

# Additional Resources

*Look on **Amazon**[30] for more specialized texts for EFT & Energy Therapy Practitioners by this author... including:*

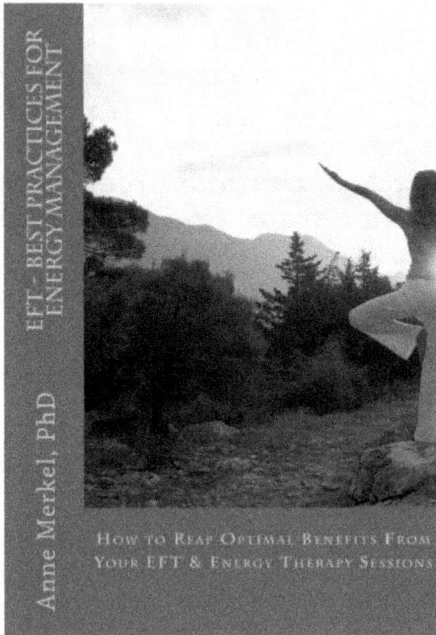

- **EFT- Best Practices for Energy Management**

---

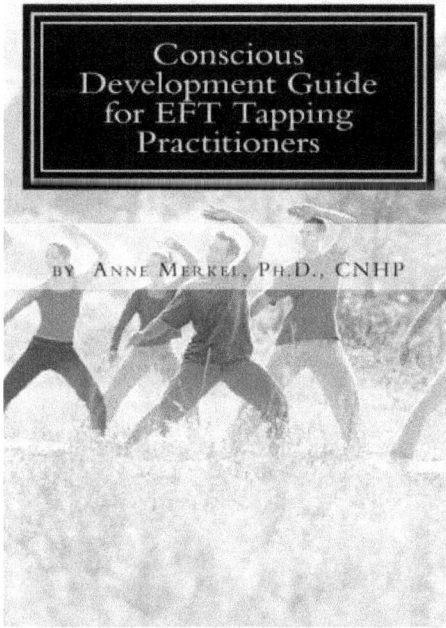

Conscious
Development Guide
for EFT Tapping
Practitioners

BY ANNE MERKEL, PH.D., CNHP

- **Transformative Coaching Guide for EFT & Energy Therapy Practitioners**

**And, if you enjoyed this book, you may also wish to check out our Wholistic Products & Services[31] .**

---

www.ingramcontent.com/pod-product-compliance
Lightning Source LLC
LaVergne TN
LVHW021457080426
835509LV00018B/2322